FRUIT

AND

VEGETABLE

ARRANGEMENTS

FRUIT AND VEGETABLE ARRANGEMENTS

EDITED BY EMMA H. CYPHERS

Hearthside Press Incorporated · Publishers · NEW YORK

CONTENTS

FRUIT

AND

VEGETABLE

ARRANGEMENTS

1

ARTISTIC APPRECIATION

OF FRUITS AND VEGETABLES

The Heritage of the Centuries Adapted to the Taste of Today

The warm and heartening response to *Holiday Flower Arrangements* has suggested a book of arrangements using fruits and vegetables. Easy to combine and with long-lasting qualities, their practical role especially on dining tables, and their use after decoration give them decorative value that can be prized throughout the year.

A potato, even the handsome apple, may not inspire a sonnet, but don't let this prevent you from seeing and enjoying the porcelain glaze of eggplant, the patterned jade of a stem of Brussels sprouts, the crowned and satin loveliness of persimmons.

Have you heard of England's first Queen Elizabeth's esteem for peas? The rarity of this legume in her day so aroused her admiration of its sleek distinctive beauty that she ordered pods showing imprisoned peas to be embroidered on her royal garment. But don't, like England's queen, enjoy only those fruits and vegetables that are diffi-

11

1 GRAPES, A PERENNIAL MOTIF *In an Early American spoon holder, the spiraled line unifies three distinct groups of plant material. A royal blue background enriches the yellow-green grapes and the violet-to-green blooms of the cup-and-saucer-vine (Cobea).* ARRANGER: MRS. LEONARD M. MATTHEWS. PHOTOGRAPHER: BOUTRELLE

cult to come by. Clear your mind of any kitchen complex, and be inspired by the inherent beauty of these familiar forms that are destined for food.

FRUIT AND VEGETABLE DECORATION THROUGH THE CENTURIES

The heritage of artistic use of fruits and vegetables is a rich one. It is believed that tendrils of the grapevine inspired the first artistic scratches on rock during the Stone Age. Ever since, man has drawn on the appeal of fruits and vegetables for decorative expression (Plate 1).

Gathering the year's harvest has always been celebrated. In early centuries, there were altars to the onion, the radish, and the cabbage with rites in honor of a deity (Plate 2). As late as the classic revival of the Renaissance, we read accounts of harvest festivals when loads of grain were capped with flowers beside an image of Demeter, Grecian goddess of sowing and reaping. To the Romans, she was Ceres.

2　"THEY OF THE GREEN AND WHITE FRUITS" *Pomona and Ceres,
mythological goddessés of fruitfulness, are inspiration for this composition. Of
particular beauty is the combination of textures in smooth translucent alabaster
figures and grapes, glossy white onions, opaque cauliflower and fleshy fungus
mushrooms.*

ARRANGER: MRS. LEONARD M. MATTHEWS.　PHOTOGRAPHER: BOUTRELLE

Even in the early Christian Era, when festivals changed in religious significance, traces of pagan customs lingered. Although early priests blessed the harvest in the churches, people in procession still carried wheat and garlands of fruit to the celebration as did their forebears. Plate 3 is contemporary decoration influenced by the symbolism of fruits in carved and painted adornment of the early Christian churches.

This symbolism was carried into the general arts as well. Because fruits hold seeds of reproduction, they were painted into garlands and swags as emblems of worthy deeds of man. Artists were commissioned to fashion fruit festoons and wreaths to beautify huge walls. Thus in the fifteenth century, Andrea della Robbia became noted for

3   A STUDY IN SYMBOLISM   *Grapes in a cluster, emblematic of unity, are arranged with other forms of Christian symbolism—pears, apples, pomegranates, ivy, and evergreen—in a container and candleholder of medieval influence. The serene and lovely Madonna completes the trinity represented in the triangle defined by candle, figure, and fruit arrangement.*
ARRANGER: MRS. CLIFFORD E. CYPHERS.   PHOTOGRAPHER: BOUTRELLE

4 RENAISSANCE CHARM *The spirit of fifteenth-century Italian enameled reliefs adorns the Christmas table and is right for the traditional or contemporary home. When just one candle is employed, a heavy one as in this arrangement is in harmony with the heaviness of fruit forms.*
ARRANGER: MRS. GEORGE GOLDSON. PHOTOGRAPHER: BRAMORE STUDIO

5 STILL LIFE *To honor friends departing for the Netherlands this decoration is reminiscent of the still-life painting of early Dutch and Flemish artists. Flowers in a period bronze container carry the eye downward in an ogee curve to a profusion of accessories completing an opulent and colorful composition.*
ARRANGER: MRS. RHYNOLD G. SCHULKE. PHOTOGRAPHER: HARRY W. SCHULKE

his enameled ceramics featuring fruits and pine cones. His name is given to this style which is popular today (Plate 4).

During the enlightened period of the Renaissance, there was increasing interest in the arts in all parts of the world. The northern European countries learned that they could grow many of those plants that were cultivated in warmer climates. To spread this new-found knowledge and wealth of ideas, Flemish and Dutch artists painted great masses of plant forms with bud, bloom, and fruit expressing the cycle of growth. Plate 5 adapts the style of this great school.

6 INSPIRATION FROM YESTERYEAR
Even a casual pile of fruit in a bowl adds color to the dining table, but how more appealing is a thoughtfully planned grouping, as in this adaptation from an early way with fruits.
ARRANGER: MRS. H. FULTON MURPHY.
PHOTOGRAPHER: OFFIE LITES

PYRAMIDS—A TABLE FASHION SINCE LONG AGO

Seventeenth-century history records the practice of placing the "noblest" form at the top of any floral grouping, and so it is not surprising to find in this position the rare and costly pineapple, which was introduced into Europe during that century. It reigned as "king of fruits" for many years, becoming an important decorative motif to symbolize hospitality on gates and fence posts, even on furniture.

Beauty for the eye while dining was appreciated even in very early times, for ancient history records the grapevine on the table "so it can be seen while tasting wine." It is natural that the high regard for the lovely pineapple should carry into dining-table decoration; it was often held aloft in a pyramid of fruits suggested in the contemporary arrangement in Plate 6. Even on the long medieval refectory tables so crowded with food that there was little room for decoration, pyramid groupings found their place. Tables were covered with cloths garlanded with fruits, flowers, and foliage that were arranged to hang over the table edge to the floor.

During the Renaissance, flowers garnished the pyramids. As time went on, great care went into their making with cushions of moss under and between each form as the pattern was built up on porcelains.

Plates 7 and 8 show the extreme standards of taste during the nineteenth century. Another fashion was to use an epergne on the table in which fruits were arranged in pyramidal symmetry in the lower sec-

7 (Left) BASKET OF PLENTY *Enjoy a Victorian basket with fruits arranged in authentic casualness. The mellow hue of natural basketry is attractive on a cloth of almost any color.*
ARRANGER: MRS. WILLIAM WHEELER.
PHOTOGRAPHER: BOUTRELLE

8 (Right) VICTORIAN SPLENDOR
Green and black grapes hung on a stick, yellow roses, springeri fern, and ivy, in an alabaster urn. With this white Ironstone china and rich gray damask fits the bountiful spirit of a table in the "plush and lush" age of the nineteenth century.
ARRANGER: MRS. WILLIAM WHEELER.
PHOTOGRAPHER: AVERILL SMITH

9 INFORMAL CHRISTMAS TEA *Inspired by the container, improvised from two reproductions of Victorian milk glass, large strawberries and small-scale lady apples are pyramided. White candles rising from miniature holly-patterned hat boxes, and red cloth and gray-green napkins to match the carnations and foliage, make a gay and feminine table.* ARRANGER: MRS. WILLIAM WHEELER. PHOTOGRAPHER: BOUTRELLE

tion with flowers in the upper (Plate 9). Earlier epergnes were designed with several wells (Plate 10) to hold only the finest and rarest fruits. These were to be looked upon only, not eaten as dessert as had been the custom.

In our own country, pyramids were used in lavish display at intervals along the length of the table. This came naturally to the gracious living of the Southern colonists; they took great pride in their privately grown greenhouse products, especially nectarines, oranges, and strawberries.

ADAPTABILITY OF FRUITS AND VEGETABLES

In today's taste for functionalism, designers turn to the abstract, the geometric, the vivid, with tendency toward texture and surface pattern. It seems logical, therefore, that the modern homemaker in

10   IN THE GRAND STYLE   *Ironstone of Chinese design, Quaker lace cloth in an early Venetian pattern, embroidered napkins of imported linen, fruit-filled silver epergne of eighteenth century England, glass candlesticks of the Victorian era, and modern Swedish crystal glasses are tastefully combined on this elegant dinner table.*
ARRANGERS: MRS. WILLIAM WHEELER; MRS. DUNHAM C. JONES.
PHOTOGRAPHER: BOUTRELLE

11 (Opposite) FUNCTIONAL MODERN
At a large picture window overlooking distant skyscrapers, this exciting table decoration was designed with the architecture of the room as a starting point. Over the osage orange at the base of tall bamboo and pale-to-deep-pink anthuriums, a green orchid corsage for the guest of honor is framed by deep green foliage and green and purple grapes.
ARRANGER: MRS. ERIC H. FEASEY.
PHOTOGRAPHER: RUSSELL LAWRENCE YOUNG

12 (Right) CASUAL AND STIMULATING *Familiar plant material in an unusual container results in an arrangement of great individuality. This intriguing decoration would lend an air of importance to an after-dinner snack table.*
ARRANGER: MRS. JAMES L. FINCH.
PHOTOGRAPHER: BOUTRELLE

search of ideas for table decoration should utilize the rigid and pronounced structural fruit and vegetable forms (Plates 11 to 14).

Because of the limitless scope of decorative possibilities that are offered by fruits and vegetables, in their infinite variety of hue, texture, and form, there can be no last word as to your choice. Exhibited throughout this book are independent and individual tastes and techniques to broaden your personal interpretation of the subject, and to show that decorating the table with fruits and vegetables is an ever-changing, continuous story.

13 (Left) WITH MODERN FLAIR *One need not use many varieties of fruits and vegetables to make a stunning arrangement. Here dramatic effect is achieved with nothing but cucumbers and aspidistra foliage. "Flowers" cut from vegetables remind us that art is a product of man, but Nature is the teacher.*
ARRANGER: MRS. HOWARD S. KITTEL.
PHOTOGRAPHER: AL ALLEMAN

14 (Below) A CHRISTMAS PLAQUE *Nuts and artificial fruits are wired to a circle cut from one-half-inch hardware mesh and attached to a hand-woven reed mat. This could be used on a bed of evergreen as table decoration or hung on the wall as a pleasing change from a picture.*
ARRANGER: MRS. LAMBERT D. LE MAIRE.
PHOTOGRAPHER: A. L. KNOWLTON-SCHEN

CHANGING THE MOOD OF A TABLE

Assuming that dishes are the unchangeable thing, it takes only color in the background linen to change the mood of a table. By way of example, study Plate 15 for possibilities. The contrast of hue afforded in the green cloth gives striking color excitement to arouse the sleepiest of sleepyheads. On a white background, the white plates with rose-red design would take on a richness well suited to more formal requirement. On a rose cloth to match the hue in the plate design, the effect would be warm, gay, and refreshingly suited to noonday dining.

15 BREAKFAST ON MOTHER'S DAY, *prepared by the two Boy Scouts in the family. Youngsters enjoy complementary hues so it is not surprising to find a green cloth as backdrop for Spode "Pink Tower" dishes. Unlike dishes are attractively mixed to harmonize. Here, white relates the Spode and unpatterned heirloom pieces—pitcher, pancake platter, irregularly-shaped butter plate, and center compote. The arrangement is topped with an orchid for mother.*
ARRANGER: MRS. LAMBERT D. LE MAIRE. PHOTOGRAPHER: A. L. KNOWLTON-SCHEN

16 STURDY FOLK ART *Hooknecked squashes repeat the gay design in "The Ploughman" plate border. Mushrooms, onions, and bananas tie in other pattern shapes. Green of textured cloth and jade plant rosettes echo the color of house and tree. Red details are echoed by radishes and apples.*
ARRANGER: MRS. H. HENRY STALEY. PHOTOGRAPHER: SCATTERGOOD STUDIO

In Plate 16, the cloth is matched to the coolest hue in the plate design to achieve a mood appropriate to dining when the temperature soars. On the other hand, by matching background cloth, mats, or doilies to the warm tone of red on the plate, an illusion of warmth would adapt the setting to cold-weather dining.

Plates 17 and 18 illustrate how a little thought can fit identical appointments to another use.

CONTINUE TRADITION WITH TODAY'S TASTES

This discussion is but a salute to the interest of mankind in artistic expression with food products, but it is enough to prove that the new

17 and 18 (Opposite) TWO WAYS WITH THE SAME APPOINTMENTS *Ivory rayon satin damask; antique flatware (pearl-handled and gold-bowled); Lenox gold-banded ivory china; antique French gilt candelabra; deep green candles; gilded fruits.*

Plate 17 shows golden-tipped arborvitae and Carolina pine with cycas leaf gilded heavily on the center rib, lightly toward the edges. Cones and lotus pods tie this material to the lovely eighteenth-century brass urn and carry the eye to gilded fruits at the base.

Plate 18 employs mugo pine lightly touched with antique gold and holly sprayed with bright gold to accent the focal area and give sparkle to the Christmas buffet. Grapes lightly-gilded reveal a hint of their natural green hue. Containers painted deep ivory and rubbed lightly with antique gold are copies of urn-shaped tops from iron Franklin stoves.
ARRANGER: MRS. RAYMOND RUSS STOLTZ. PHOTOGRAPHER: ARTHUR HEITZMAN

19 TRADITIONAL WITH CONTEMPORARY ACCENT *The wreath of holly, large berried juniper, small cones and cream-hued cedar is embellished with corsages of the same materials, one for each guest at a Christmas luncheon. A red candle illuminates with cheer and symbolism.*
WREATH: MR. CARL STARKER. CORSAGES: MRS. WARDER IRWIN HIGGINS.
PHOTOGRAPHER: C. OWEN SMITHERS

is often very old. You can continue as tradition dictates, but with adaptation to present-day taste and standards. Plates 19 and 20 are a reminder that decorative design with fruits and vegetables can be scaled and colored to suit contemporary living.

20 RICH AND FORMAL BEAUTY *A beautiful antique silver epergne is inspiration to display the most exquisite forms and textures obtainable. Here are included such beauties as green pears, mottled reddish-brown pears, chartreuse Italian peppers, red and yellow lady apples, red strawberries, red, blue, purple grapes combined with ivy and gardenia foliage, and flower buds.*
ARRANGER: MRS. ROBERT NATHAN GRAHAM. PHOTOGRAPHER: THE ALBERT STUDIO

2

COMPATIBILITY OF THE

TABLE DECORATION

*Forms, Hues, Textures of Fruits and Vegetables; Formality or Informality,
Containers*

If we were to discuss fruits and vegetables in the language of the
botanist, we would find that the terms would differ from popular
conception and use. Too much discrimination in terms would over-
load a book on decoration, so for our purpose it will be enough to
establish description of our fruits and vegetables as "edible food for
man." Thus we include such things as the mushroom (a fungus), the
corn (a grass), the fig (a flower receptacle).

THE IMPORTANT FORMS OF FRUITS AND VEGETABLES

Compared to flowers, fruits and vegetables are relatively simple in
shape. Some, such as the pear and carrot, are conelike; some, like the

28

orange, are round; others, such as the turnip and squash, are a combination of both. Those with a well-defined flat surface are cubical; the banana and pomegranate are typical of this form. This geometrical aspect provides classic and architectural solidity to our medium. For the most part, the forms seem designed to be looked *upon*, although the leaf and "head" types, like so many flowers, have an intimate appeal better appreciated when looked *into*.

Plate 21 indicates the special advantage of this "solid" quality in decoration when planned for the modern low table from which refreshments are sometimes served in the living room or on the porch or terrace.

FORMS, HUES, AND TEXTURES DENOTE FORMALITY OR INFORMALITY

Nature endows our medium with unsurpassable hue, but texture is even more significant. Variety runs the gamut from the downy surface

21 SEPTEMBER THEME   *Squashes, pumpkins, strawberry corn, and wheat are texturally right in this uncomplicated pattern of forms, in some respects alike, in others quite different.*
ARRANGER AND PHOTOGRAPHER: MRS. H. B. ISOM.

22 TO COMPLEMENT THE TABLE *On a beautiful mantel of marble and muted pistachio-green against a wall of delicate violet-gray this antique gold-framed mirror and black marble urns are favorite Christmas decoration. To echo gold bas-relief on the standards, acorn squashes in the urns are touched with gold paint. Rust to violet-red Tokay grapes and clusters of pittosporum add variety.* ARRANGER: MRS. RAYMOND RUSS STOLTZ. PHOTOGRAPHER: ARTHUR HEITZMAN

of the peach to the hard smooth shine of the pepper; from the dullness of the potato to the oblique striping of the pineapple and the patterned shells of many varieties of nuts.

Similar to flowers and foliage, fruits and vegetables may be formal or informal to fit the type of table linen, glassware, and dishes, the occasion for the setting, and the room in which the table is prepared. By way of example, the rugged potato is casual, unceremonious, and informal as compared to the refined finish and precise form of a glossy eggplant. As compared with the dainty lady apple, the russet variety is informal. Red cabbage with its silky sheen is of greater dignity than the ordinary type. Red bananas give a greater feeling of refinement than the more common yellow. Limes seem more delicate than lemons. In general, such exotic forms as the prickly pear and pomegranate are of more formal character than practical varieties of home-grown crops.

COMPATIBILITY WITH ANY TYPE OF DINING ROOM

Because the character of our medium ranges from delicacy to boldness, casualness to formality, you can plan your decoration to

23 (Right) A REFLECTIVE MOOD *Taking her cue from an elegant bronze candlestick, the arranger has maintained symmetry without rigid repetition (note variety in the holder's pattern). Aware that composition is more than rule, she has achieved an appropriate and flexible center-placement arrangement. On one side of the candlestick, silky African-silvertree foliage extends across the marbleized base with red grapes as center of interest. On the other, pears and lady apples meet the eye.*

ARRANGER: MRS. SAMUEL LASKER.

PHOTOGRAPHER: BOUTRELLE-SEVECKE

24 (Below) CHARMING SUPPER TABLE *Dainty white organdy mats, handblown goblets with crystal stems and amethyst bowls (compatible with purple grapes on the lustre plates) and oval glass platter containers, are in harmony on this party table. Rhythmic patterns of Scotch broom are stabilized at the base with purple grapes and andromeda foliage. White candles decorated with grapes and leaves of colored wax, add a sumptuous note.*

ARRANGER: MRS. DOROTHY M. HINMAN.

PHOTOGRAPHER: BOUTRELLE

25 VACATION MEMORIES *To complement Mexican wood carvings in a
restful pose, a simple and static pyramidal form is defined by maguey leaves
(century plant). Set towards the back of a container constructed from brown
stained plywood, they give height. Banana flowers, mahogany-red and yellow in
color, supply intermediate and foreground planes, with small yellow-green bananas carrying the eye to the sleeping figurines.*
ARRANGER: MRS. ALBERT P. MICCICHE.   PHOTOGRAPHER: AL ALLEMAN

26 EXCITING DIAGONAL *Arresting and active diagonal lines dominate this design, composed as an asymmetrical triangle. To counteract the tendency of a diagonal to move the eye out of the picture, destroying unity, contrast is supplied in light and dark grapes . . . of sufficient force to balance the oblique placement of ti leaves. Looped foliage is held in place with common pins.*

ARRANGER: MRS. HOWARD MC CLELLAND.

PHOTOGRAPHER: RICCI STUDIO

harmonize with familiar everyday furnishings and accessories and the room as a whole (Plates 22, 23, 24, 25). With early American furniture and table appointments, you might design a casual grouping of native forms in browns, reds, and yellows in an appropriate container —perhaps a metal tray, an old sugar scoop, or salt box.

In a sophisticated atmosphere, you would prefer a stylized design with the emphasis on well-polished forms (Plate 26).

27 TRADITIONAL SOUTHERN HOSPITALITY *Surrounding hues are mirrored in the gleaming silver samovar from the famed old Williams House in Montmorency, South Carolina. Southern broom, boxwood, pittosporum, and loquat are highlighted with camellias. Grapes, limes, yellow apples, nectarines, plums, and clusters of green foliage at the base echo their value and tone contrasts. (Part of this home, purchased by Harry DuPont, can be seen in Wilmington today.)*

ARRANGER: MRS. WILLIAM WHEELER.

PHOTOGRAPHER: BOUTRELLE

28 FOR A CHURCH SUPPER *Harvest from a garden provides buttercup and hooked-necked squashes, a pepper, and tomatoes in variety, combined with funkia (hosta) and iris leaves to develop a triangular pattern. Long-ribbed okra pods add texture and shape interest. Though these are dried and beyond the stage of taste perfection, they rival any ornamental garden plant with their yellow flowers, abundant foliage, and edible green pods as bonus!*
ARRANGER: MRS. O. C. WENBORG.
PHOTOGRAPHER: MINNEAPOLIS STAR & TRIBUNE

In the especially elegant room, nothing surpasses silver in which to arrange fruits (Plate 27). If grapes are included, their covering of a powdery substance or "bloom," giving a grayish tone, relates the hue of the silver to the grouping of mixed forms.

A combination of green peppers, red apples, yellow squashes, and green grapes fits a dining room in either a blended or a contrasted color scheme (Plate 28).

In a room of pastel coloring, and on a table set with fine linen and china in delicate coloring, you will enjoy a one-hue blend, such as "fragile" green grapes, small limes, and green apples.

CONTAINERS EMPHASIZE CHARACTER OF DECORATION

Versatile fruits and vegetables are rugged enough to be used in wood, and yet distinctive enough with silver (Plates 20, 27). Generally speaking, good basic containers give a substantial appearance suited to accommodating the feeling of weight in our medium. Metal plates

29 (Opposite) FOR PICNIC PARTIES *Description of this informal grouping can best be summed up as "studied carelessness". Rose-hued crab apples in little bunches as they grow, and grapes spill casually over the edge of a miniature huckster barrow. Zinnias (pale to deep pink) are scaled from small to large to meet tomatoes in the cart.*
ARRANGER: MRS. EDWIN L. HOLT.   PHOTOGRAPHER: WAYNE ADAMS

30 CASUAL CHARM *Color and scale are stressed in this combination of red grapes and apples, yellow pears, and laurel foliage on an antique pewter hot-water plate. One sees things important in a well-organized fruit-vegetable arrangement: dominance of hue, value, texture; interesting variation; rhythmic size gradation. For harmony and unity, bloom on grapes and apples repeats pewter-gray; crescent design echoes plate contour. The open area rests the eye and prevents heaviness.*

ARRANGER: MRS. E. B. HEADDEN.   PHOTOGRAPHER: HORACE SHELDON

and trays, heavy pottery, wooden receptacles, low bowls harmonize with informal combinations of robust varieties (Plates 30, 31). Polished metal, particularly silver, heavy glass, china containers of the compote type (Plate 15) present an elegance in line with out-of-season delicacies, the hard-to-get varieties. They are well suited when tribute is paid to one fruit as in Plate 32.

31 EARLY SUMMER COMBINATION *Small green bananas, young green apples, limes, succulents, red cherries, and copper beach foliage arranged on a wooden tray present a lush and handsome ensemble.*

ARRANGER: MRS. GEORGE J. HIRSCH.   PHOTOGRAPHER: MICHAEL G. SPOTO

32 ACCENT ON THE ORANGE *Even an ordinary fruit goes aristocratic when arranged to display its most flattering aspect. Here dominance of hue, texture, and shape of oranges in variety are emphasized in a black bowl. Elegant greenhouse foliage adds to the quality of refinement though the design is unceremoniously asymmetrical. Copper tones on the variegated leaves are repeated in the base.*

ARRANGER: MRS. ARTHUR P. ZUCK.   PHOTOGRAPHER: BRYAN STUDIO

Cornucopias (Plate 33) are extremely decorative. When empty, they may seem elaborate, but when forms are combined in them to follow the rhythm of their long sweeping line, they appear to be comparatively simple receptacles. Since they are made of various substances, there will always be one for your particular need.

Iron receptacles (Plates 34, 69) have an aptitude for combining with all fruits and vegetables. They are neutral in the sense that texture is not important. They have no grain to dominate as has

33 GAY AND SPRINGLIKE *Though more generally used in the harvest theme, a cornucopia is adaptable to springtime decoration for the spring goddess, Flora, is represented in art carrying it filled with flowers and fruits. The "horn of plenty" is particularly fitting filled to overflowing with products of a rejuvenated Nature. In this decoration foliage, blossom, and fruit of strawberry are combined with kale and ivy to encompass the year's cycle of growth in a sweeping pattern like that of the container itself.*
ARRANGER: MRS. C. D. BERGSTROM.
PHOTOGRAPHER: HELLER-GADEKE STUDIO

34 IN A PAIR OF CONTAINERS EMPLOYED AS ONE *Planned for a table against the wall, this modern pattern has solidity of arrangement without sacrificing liveliness, supplied here by the "linear" candle holders. Can you envision the soft reflection of candle glow in the lustrous fruit?*
ARRANGER: MRS. GEORGE GOLDSON.   PHOTOGRAPHER: BRAMORE STUDIO

35 TO PROVOKE A MOOD A *woven reed bottle holder supports a gay springtime arrangement of young crisp rhubarb leaves, asparagus, and strawberries. The cap of the basket, in cornucopia style, spills onions, new potatoes, mushrooms, broccoli, radishes, and new peas in their pods onto a mat of woven palm, to produce a novel and interesting composition rich in revelation of a mood.* ARRANGER: MRS. JAMES L. FINCH. PHOTOGRAPHER: BOUTRELLE

wood, and no obtrusive color. I have seen them combined satis-
factorily with straw, glass, wood, and even marble.

Baskets are versatile containers and an item of collection for the
arranger (Plates 35, 36, 37). Woven of some product of nature, such
as willow, grasses, corn husks, leaves or strips of palm or of wood,
their diversified shapes, weaves, and textures range from the very
primitive to the most sophisticated, and each style demands that its
individuality be stressed in the plant material and design used in it.
Even the lowly chip basket piled with garden products pays off in
aesthetic dividend.

36 CHAFING DISH OR COFFEE KLATSCH FUN *When impromptu*
refreshments are required, fruits and vegetables in a basket are quick and easy
decoration. Entertainment of this sort is so little trouble and so much fun if
you plug in the coffee, heat foods in a chafing dish at the table, and design an
arrangement such as this to lend warm and friendly atmosphere.
ARRANGER: MRS. C. D. BERGSTROM.   PHOTOGRAPHER: HELLER-GADEKE STUDIO

37 "OH, WHAT A BEAUTIFUL MORNING" *The simplest appointments become impressive when thoughtfully combined. A handleless lacy-weave
basket ties dainty shapes and hues to details in heirloom furniture. Brown in the
plate is echoed by brown glasses, fruit cups, napkins, and tile. Cream tone of
reed mats and yellows in the arrangement pick up the design on Majolica coffee
pot. Curves are dominant; scalloped edges of plates are in tune with leaves of the
brown-pegged cherry table. Variation is introduced in the squares of ash tray,
sugar, creamer, and tile to achieve the epitome of art—repetition plus variety.*
ARRANGERS: MRS. ALFRED S. GRUSSNER; MRS. LAMBERT D. LE MAIRE.
PHOTOGRAPHER: A. L. KNOWLTON-SCHEN

FIND INTERESTING CONTAINERS IN YOUR HOME

You can find interesting containers on your kitchen shelf if you rid
your mind of prejudice. If you have inexpensive chopping bowls in a
variety of sizes, choose two in pleasing proportion to each other. Turn
the smaller upside down, and glue the bottom of the larger to it—

presto, a standard-type receptacle of charm. (Plate 38). Or glue two of the same size, bottoms together, and stand upright on the table. Combine vegetables against the inside of each to spill out on a base.

On a small table, a glass goblet upside down makes a novel pedestal to support a large, glistening Spanish onion. To prevent toppling off, secure it to the glass with floral clay. I am quite prepared to be laughed at, but try it! The effect will amaze you.

Even an empty fish tank challenges. Try an underwater decoration. Select a few heavily veined, beautifully fringed kale leaves that would rise no farther than an inch or so from the tank's rim. Arrange them on a pin-holder, and submerge them to achieve a dramatic picture that is quite cooling on a hot summer's day. After a few hours, the kale becomes jeweled with an edging of tiny bubbles and remains lovely to look at for at least three days. Such treatment of familiar material may be just the thing to open your eyes to "beauty in common things." Or substitute a cabbage for the kale. First allow cold water from the faucet to run over the head to encourage leaves to curl away from the solid center.

38 NOVEMBER IN GEORGIA *Unlike other orchard trees persimmons drop leaves before fruit has ripened and the bright red-orange balls silhouetted against a blue sky inspire November decoration. Design is on three levels. A slender brass pitcher holds tall placement; wooden bowls, one inverted, make a second; a single wooden bowl, the third.*
ARRANGER: MRS. HENRY R. PERKINS.   PHOTOGRAPHER: MORGAN FITZ

39 "COOKED BY THE SUN" *is the meaning of pumpkin, derived from a Greek word. Its golden hue is the symbol of sun, of power, of glory. In the fall when the earth abounds with hues that reflect the light of a constant sun, a blemish-free pumpkin is a fitting container. Its top as accessory is a "touch that tells".*

ARRANGER: MRS. LOUIS H. AMER.   PHOTOGRAPHER: CARPENTER'S STUDIO

40 BLACK MAGIC HALLOWEEN *In the spirit of Halloween a black bust with coral and gilt turban sets a witchcraft theme. A gray-brown coconut holds weird driftwood, gray-green succulent foliage, gilded pods, and coral-colored chrysanthemums lightly touched with gilt. Lipstick on the dried gourd stains it coral. In a room with gray-green background, this arrangement would be a daring accent.* ARRANGER: MRS. ALBERT P. MICCICHE. PHOTOGRAPHER: ELEANOR MORGAN

NATURAL CONTAINERS—FRUITS, VEGETABLES, BARK, STUMPS, ROOTS

To use a natural fruit or vegetable as container, as illustrated in Plates 39 and 40, select one that will stand securely upright. Cut or saw off the top, and scoop out the seeds. An inserted bowl of water will keep the flowers and foliage fresh, although woody branches will remain so simply by sharpening the stem ends and pushing them directly into the moist flesh, as in a pumpkin or eggplant.

Or a large piece of bark, as in Plate 41, will excite admiration. A large fungus is a possibility. It can be preserved for years by storing it away with moth-preventive crystals when it is not in use. Perhaps a tree stump (Plate 42) or a root segment will fire your imagination (Plate 43).

41 A BREEZEPROOF ARRANGEMENT *Out-of-doors, natural table accessories are exceptionally interesting. On a terrace barbecue table, fruits and vegetables seem at home in a bark container. To assemble bold and positive forms in a pattern such as here—neither too rigid, nor too loose and untidy—requires skill and understanding. A pineapple supplies an attractive upswing line.*

ARRANGER: MRS. GEORGE GOLDSON. PHOTOGRAPHER: BRAMORE STUDIO

42 FOR COUNTRY LIVING *Rural folks relish a drink made by soaking in water red sumac berries (only the gray and white are poisonous). And the wilding plaintain, parent of our garden funkia, has long been enjoyed as a vegetable green . . . so this decoration is appropriate for our book of edible fruits and vegetables. It would be fun to replace the pine and sumac on the plaque with bright red apples, to pay tribute to Johnny Appleseed, who scattered appleseeds and sermons as he traveled the byways of the midwest.*

ARRANGER: MRS. LOUIS H. AMER.

PHOTOGRAPHER: EDWARD NAHER

Find such suitable stumps and roots in the woods—remains of trees felled many years ago and weathered until there is nothing left but a shell-like structure. Prepare the treasures with care to render them clean and attractive for table use. Cut away any undesirable debris or awkward angles with a knife. Wash thoroughly, and when dry, finish by one of the following methods to give hardness to surfaces that long exposure to the elements has made soft and porous. Rub carefully with pumice stone and linseed oil, with fine emery paper, or with #000 mineral wool. Now wax to harmonize with maple furniture or to fit a ranch-type home, or paint with varnish wood stain to give refinement in keeping with fine-grained mahogany or walnut furnishings, then wax.

43 FOR AN OPEN-AIR SUPPER *Add a citronella candle between radishes and grapefruit not only for height but to discourage insects; its odor is in offensive in the open. The container is part of a hollowed root segment from which the outer surface has been removed to expose a soft rosy-red heart.*
ARRANGER: MRS. CLIFFORD E. CYPHERS.   PHOTOGRAPHER: CHARLES F. CYPHERS

44 (Left) FAR AWAY PLACES As container, a fiber mat is secured to a cylindrical receptacle, a fitting companion in pattern, texture, and hue for the natural sea fan which gives meaning to green-bronze "fish-in-a-wave" accessories. Against a forest-green background, green-white calla lily buds and freesias combine with white edged pandanus foliage (looped and pinned to hold position), rubber-plant leaves, and limes.

ARRANGER: MRS. LEROY BANKS.

PHOTOGRAPHER: BOUTRELLE

45 (Right) PLAID CLOTHES FOR GAIETY On a lively blue with green, violet, and white cloth, plain napkins and simple appointments are appropriate. The container, cleverly assembled by screwing together a central section of an antique Lincoln stove, is painted green and rubbed with umber to soften the finish. Candle bases are wrapping-paper rollers, notched and painted to harmonize. Candles are toned by mixing green and blue bronzing powder and applying it with cheesecloth.

ARRANGER: MRS. SAMUEL LASKER.

PHOTOGRAPHER: BOUTRELLE-SEVECKE

Once you set your mind to it, you will think of many receptacle possibilities that will tag your arrangement as original. Never forget that the value of a jewel is arbitrary except to you—the worth is your own estimate. Who can tell the value of a container you have made yourself! (Plates 44, 45, 62, 84).

46 SET FOR INFORMAL ENTERTAIN-
ING *Two coconut spathes curved at the
ends serve as a base in this decoration appropriately designed for use when place settings are on only three sides of a table. Varied
colored gourds, grapes, limes are in accord
with the chartreuse cloth and two-color dishes.
Handmade candles pick up the hue of spathes
and wooden monk.*
ARRANGER: MRS. H. HENRY STALEY.
PHOTOGRAPHER: SCATTERGOOD STUDIO

47 (Opposite) SIDE-TABLE DECORA-
TION *A large palmetto leaf selected for
its undulating pattern supports southern fruits
highlighted with gladiolus blooms and buds.
Among them are several carambolas, the
orange-yellow opalescent "starfruits" of Flor-
ida. Unfortunately this sweet variety is rare.
Cut crosswise into thin slices, they are starlike
shapes to embellish any fruit punch, and to
add delightful flavor.*
ARRANGER: MRS. CLIFFORD E. CYPHERS.
PHOTOGRAPHER: CHARLES F. CYPHERS

But use such ingenious containers discreetly for even a wonderful
idea can lose its interest with unrestrained repetition. The one fault
with really distinctive arrangements is that they often produce a great
number of bad imitations.

PLAQUES, STANDS, BASES

If fruits and/or vegetables are combined without the limitation im-
posed by a container, arrange them on a base to prevent possible stain
to the table surface or cover. A coconut spathe as in Plate 46 is effective. Or use a foundation of one large fresh leaf (Plate 47). But a
wood base is more substantial, allowing easy removal of the decoration (intact) when there is need to change the table setting. A slab
of wood—natural, polished, or stained—is useful (Plates 48, 49).

48 "CAJUN COUNTRY" HARVEST FESTIVAL *In the Pelican state where sweet potatoes became economically important when cotton crops failed years ago, a picturesque fête, known to Louisianans as "Yambilee", is held annually, followed by the Sugar Cane Festival. To honor these events sweet potatoes, its foliage, and jointed iridescent stalks of sugar cane are combined to follow the lively pattern of the crescent.*
ARRANGER: MRS. JOHN STEGEN.   PHOTOGRAPHER: AL ALLEMAN

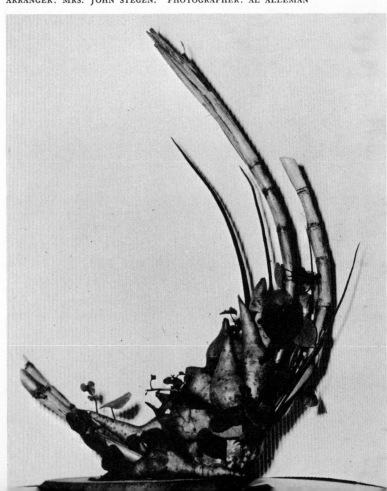

49 (Above) GOURMET'S DELIGHT

Against a wine-red cloth, a polished wooden plaque holds pineapple, peppers, florets of broccoli, brown-skinned onions, artichokes, limes, zucchini squashes, a red-purple cabbage, a hand of brown-red Jamaica bananas, and Tokay grapes. Edam cheese, in its red wrapper, and a duck, add meaning to the theme.

ARRANGER: MRS. JOHN COOPER GRAHAM

PHOTOGRAPHER: BOUTRELLE

50 (Left) GAY DECORATION FOR AN OUTDOOR MEAL

A pleasing proportion, balance, and harmony of line, form, and color display the skill of this arranger in decoration that is a tribute to her "seeing eye." Arranged on slate, shapes of osage oranges, grapes, and rosette-like echeveria reflect the loveliness of manzanita beautifully sculptured by Nature.

ARRANGER: MRS. C. C. THACH.

PHOTOGRAPHER: BOUTRELLE

52 (Below) FRUIT AND FLOWERS FOR EASTER BEAUTY *Arranged for a marble-top chest, this restrained arrangement evokes a quiet joy in the underlying spirit of Easter. It is a potential sculptor who would combine strong line, definite shape, and firm texture with a solidity of design to create a mood. Symbolic color cooperates with the Easter mood.*
ARRANGER: MRS. HOWARD MC CLELLAND.
PHOTOGRAPHER: RICCI STUDIO

51 (Above) WITH AESTHETIC APPEAL *The glory of autumn is caught in this attractive combination on a base polished to a soft patina echoed in much of these fruit and vegetable forms. By contrast, the comparatively dull surface of squashes emphasize refined finishes. Texture of pomegranates, like smooth leather, is transition between the two extremes. Note how forms are turned to lead the eye easily through the design.*
ARRANGER: MRS. JOHN COOPER GRAHAM.
PHOTOGRAPHER: BOUTRELLE

Bamboo stands are popular (Plate 83). Flat stone or slate is particularly proper when the table is set in a corner of the garden (Plate 50). Stands of fine-grained wood, such as mahogany, ebony, or teakwood, are more elegant in character (Plate 51).

In many pictures in this book, you will see that even under a container a base supplies finesse if it is chosen to harmonize in size, in shape, in hue, and in texture. Irregular contour in slabs of wood, in their natural state or polished or painted, fit the primitive designs. Disks, squares, and rectangles are suited to the style of dignity. Plinths are especially fitting with a pattern of grandeur (Plate 52).

3

GROOMING FRUITS

AND VEGETABLES

Plant Material Must Be Clean, Crisp, and Blemish-free for Pleasure and for Lasting Quality

The dining table is a background for eating so have nothing unappetizing in its decoration. Unless you plan to stress exceptional beauty of just one fruit or vegetable, horticultural perfection is not a requisite. Sometimes irregularities prove intriguing and undersized forms may be in better scale as the diminutive pumpkin in Plate 53 reveals.

53 (Opposite) ARTFULLY SIMPLE *This competitive flower-show exhibit is reproduced to illustrate a harvest theme in a garden setting. An old wooden salt box overflows in horn-of-plenty fashion onto a yellow textured cloth. Brown and green earthenware casseroles on deep yellow pottery plates and amber glasses are effective in this informal setting.*
ARRANGER: MRS. JAMES L. FINCH.   PHOTOGRAPHER: BOUTRELLE

POLISHING AND HARDENING TO ENHANCE PLANT MATERIAL

Polishing solid fruits and vegetables removes the natural waxy film that preserves and gives characteristic texture, but on the other hand soft cloth polishing lightens highlights.

Harden leafy vegetables (as chard) by complete submersion in water for several hours before arranging them. Before soaking, split the stem end of thick-ribbed varieties (as kale) to aid absorption of water. It is not advisable to store in the refrigerator during the soaking period.

TIMING NECESSARY IN PICKING AND IN MARKET SELECTION

Some fruits and vegetables require picking before they are fully matured if they are to last in decoration. Racemes of cherry tomatoes are an example; fruits drop quickly at prime development.

Ordinary tomatoes cut in the spray are irresistible, but these too must be underripe. You can control placement better in arrangement if you wire the succulent stem, heavy with red or yellow tomatoes, to a twig for support.

Elderberries last well if you pick their branches just as the fruit begins to color. Then too, the unusual overlay of bronzy purple on green is particularly pleasing.

Beauty of unripened material often rivals that of the fully matured. In our Southland, I have marveled at an effect similar to a pattern of Chinese art as persimmons on light brown branches, indoors in a vase, changed from gray-green to yellow-gold, then to vermilion.

If your choice of decorative material is from the store bin, the underripe is generally preferable. This is especially so with yellow bananas. Your palate may relish the ripe, brown-specked fruit, but its odor can be offensive. Select them with tips still green. Even in the

54 (Opposite) GREEN FOR MARCH   *A hand of green bananas is the interest area around which papyrus, fruit of pandanus (screw pine)—with its ribbon-striped yellow and green curled leaves repeating the growth pattern of the branch —yellow spotted hothouse foliage, and a manzanita branch are skillfully grouped to produce an intriguing silhouette on a mahogany board.*
ARRANGER: MRS. JESSE FORT.   PHOTOGRAPHER: WARBECK STUDIO

all-green stage, they can add a quality of the unusual to your grouping (Plate 54).

Examine the stem of grape clusters. If it has begun to shrivel and lose its greenness, the bunch will shatter in handling.

NATURE FAKING

Apply a "blushing cheek," as lovely as any Nature paints, with lip-stick smoothed with your finger on the too-green or too-yellow apple or pear. If your need is a sweeping line, such as grapes give to design, at a time when fresh fruit is not suited to your plan, wire tiny forms into grape-like clusters. Pickling onions, radishes, tiny baby potatoes are easy to manage. Small nuts, too, as almonds, chestnuts, pecans, are worth the time required to complete a "bunch." An example is seen in Plate 87.

To do this, drill a hole completely through the nut toward the stem end. Pull a length of wire through each, and group them into bunches, twisting the wires to secure them so.

And artificial fruits are feasible. They are so beautifully made today that they are fast gaining favor among decorators. They are used with appreciation in Plates 55 and 86.

ORNAMENTAL FRUITS—GOURDS, CONES, AND OSAGE ORANGE

Though the great family of gourds includes the many varieties of melons, some of its members are but ornamental, and according to our definition are not representative of either fruit or vegetable. They are, nevertheless, agreeable companions to our medium, so it is not amiss to discuss their charm. They can be grown in an astounding diversity of hue, texture, and shape (Plate 56).

Advice on harvesting and preserving them varies. I suggest that you cut them from the vine in late fall, but before frost. Leave at least a two-inch stem attached; it is attractive and seems to aid preservation. Dry them in a cool room allowing each gourd free exposure to air. In two weeks, apply an insecticide (any will do) to prevent fungus growth on the surface. About January, give a final coating of either varnish, shellac, or liquid wax to keep the gourds for months. I prefer the latter, as it brings out natural coloring and its soft luster is unobtrusive.

55 A BOW TO SWEDEN *Wheat, pine, artificial fruits and leaves in yellows, golds, and blues adorn a tray of woven palm. Peasant dolls, made by the arranger, repeat blue and gold (symbolic of Sweden). It is plausible to substitute fresh fruit in this type of decoration; shellac coating will preserve them for at least two weeks.*
ARRANGER: MRS. WILLIAM E. SEIBEL.
PHOTOGRAPHER: BRYAN STUDIO

For a novel fruit, withhold the mold preventive, thus encouraging a finely mottled pattern to develop on the surface. Lasting quality is impaired, but elegance compensates for shorter life. A large pear-shaped gourd so affected, displayed upright on a hand-carved teak-wood stand, is extremely handsome.

The wrinkly skinned chartreuse osage orange of the spiny "hedge tree" is inedible too, but because of compatibility with our medium should not be ignored (Plate 57). It falls to the ground in autumn and lasts many weeks without shriveling or decaying. I have kept several in an airtight jar in my refrigerator for months, using them at intervals in winter decoration.

The richly patterned cones of needled evergreen trees should not go unsung. These ornamentals offer texture, contrasting smooth surfaces in Plate 58. Gather them at almost any time during the year. Wash ground dirt from them, and they are ready to embellish an

56 CONSIDER THE ORNAMENTAL GOURDS *Gourds in various hues,*
textures, and shapes combine in "unity within variety." The brass candelabrum
and tray are texturally right; dark-green candles repeat the hue of ivy leaves.
Leucothoe serves as transition between the low placement of gourds and high
candles.

ARRANGER: MRS. LOUIS H. AMER.   PHOTOGRAPHER: CARPENTER'S STUDIO

57 IT'S THE BERRIES *Even in early summer you can use berries, for loose racemes of rose-purple berries of wild shadbush or June-berry can be arranged in a style similar to this composition of pyracantha berries. And they are delicious to human taste either fresh or dried. Early yellow apples could replace the osage oranges.*
ARRANGER: MRS. WILLIAM E. SEIBEL.
PHOTOGRAPHER: BRYAN STUDIO

arrangement at any time; they keep forever. Newly fallen cones have the look of unpolished wood. If they have weathered to become dark and unattractive, gild, silver, or bronze them for use when such a touch is appropriate.

ARTIFICIALLY COLORED MATERIAL

Do not hesitate to color plant material artificially. If so treated, it may be more consistent with a personal innovation appropriate to a special event, occasion, or expression (Plates 55, 59). Use a paint-brush to apply house paint or bronzing liquid. Bronzing powder and liquid can be purchased separately in hardware or art supply stores. If you plan to use gold, add a pinch of silver powder or a bit of brown water paint to the gold to reduce "brassiness" to a soft lustrous gold finish.

DRIED FRUITS AND VEGETABLES

In California, dried vegetables threaded into a "charm spray" are popular wall adornment, especially in the breakfast nook. And one cannot visit Mexico without being impressed with the long, thin, dried red peppers strung together and hung as welcome notes at

58 SYMMETRY AND REFINEMENT *A wooden container bought for almost nothing in a Thrift Shop is touched with gold to suggest the richness of a Renaissance piece. Colorful fruit and foliage arranged with the delicacy of a gracefully-curved pattern are just right with the character of this container.*
ARRANGER: MRS. ROBERT STRAUB.   PHOTOGRAPHER: BOUTRELLE-SEVECKE

59 CARNIVAL SPIRIT *Dried plant material including globe artichokes on false stems is arranged to frame dull black ceramic masks on black glass stands. Such "spook glamour" on a refreshment table would induce each guest to unleash his spirit and join in the fun of Halloween whoopie.*

ARRANGER: MRS. HERBERT BLUMBERG.
PHOTOGRAPHER: HERBERT BACHRACH

home entrances. Hot peppers such as these and usable strings of dried onions are available at Italian grocers, and many dehydrated interesting forms are discovered in Chinese markets, but it is fun to dry your own fruits and vegetables. No special method is required; only time in a cool room with each piece exposed to a free circulation of air.

After about three months, the pomegranate shrinks to emphasize its cubical form; the color remains almost as vivid as in the fresh state. I have enjoyed a citrus orange which dried quite by accident. Its resultant red-brown paper-like texture is entirely different from that of any other plant form known to me. In the drying process, the greenness of globe artichokes takes on a brownish tone, and the bud opens or spreads somewhat.

THE POMANDER OR SPICE BALL

Though it was the ancient Egyptians who discovered the keeping quality of cloves, it was our grandmothers who applied the knowledge to preserving fruit as "spice balls." A correctly made pomander

60 SPOTLIGHT ON DRIED FRUITS AND VEGETABLES *This amaz-
ing assemblage of dried forms described on page 64 is a sure bet to pique curi-
osity and stimulate around-the-table conversation. The linen is rich brown; plate
is heavy pottery; glass has a processed texture of lattice pattern harmonizing with
the texture of the woven palm mat.*
ARRANGER: MRS. SIMEON TAYLOR SHIELDS.
PHOTOGRAPHER: MRS. C. COLTON TUTTLE

retains its spicy fragrance and lasts indefinitely, eventually becoming
petrified.

Here is the process for making it to supply texture variation in
arrangement. Start with a well-shaped apple or thin-skinned orange
of medium size. Wash and dry it thoroughly. Now rub it gently with
a greased cloth. Circle the stem of the fruit with cloves pushed in up
to their patterned heads. Follow with row after row until the fruit
is *completely* crusted. Now roll it in a mixture of one teaspoon of
powdered orrisroot and one of cinnamon. Wrap the ball in waxed
paper to dry, and store for at least a week in any out-of-the-way
corner of your kitchen or workshop. Remove the paper, brush off
excess powder, and your pomander is ready for decorative use. One
or two are sufficient in a fruit-vegetable arrangement; if too many are
combined, the fragrance may be overpowering.

61 **A UNION OF DRIED AND FRESH** *Varying lengths in embryo palm set the silhouette for this combination of eggplant, grapes, plums, rose camellias, and angel wing begonia foliage. Character is determined by dominance of fresh plant material; subordination of dried palm serves as any well-organized element of contrast—that is, to enrich the dominant feature.*

ARRANGER: MRS. H. FULTON MURPHY. PHOTOGRAPHER: W. A. NILES

EXPERIMENT IN DRYING AND PRESERVING

If you enjoy experimenting, you'll be amazed at what can be achieved in drying and preserving fruits and vegetables. One arranger's experiments are seen in Plate 60. Against a large curved-neck gourd, the eye-catching and uplifting agency is of wheat ears and corn tassels strengthening the sweep of wistaria. Deep red-brown dulse (dried seaweed eaten for rich iodine content) brings emphasis at its logical location low near the area where plant material and bamboo raft meet. Attention is directed here by onions (only an ethereal red-tan silky shell remains after six months of drying), eggplant slices (selected at a Chinese grocery for pierced design and pewter-like texture and hue), plantain (an edible leaf from the wild), nasturtium foliage (a zippy salad ingredient), and the purple-black and claw-like hooded flower of skunk cabbage (relished by the Red Man).

Even if you are one who has an aversion to anything other than fresh-cut plant material on the dining table, you cannot deny the fascination of interesting dried forms, used occasionally, combined with fresh as in Plate 61.

FOR THE BUFFET *Appealing to eye and palate, watermelon wedges in a glass bowl keep refreshingly cool with ice cubes. A pretty idea, easy to do and practical, for fruit serves as dessert as well as decoration on your summer buffet.*
ARRANGER: ANN HAGAN.   PHOTOGRAPHER: WILLIAM HOWLAND   COURTESY: GOOD HOUSEKEEPING MAGAZINE

4

THE TECHNIQUE

OF ARRANGEMENT

Pleasing Relationship of All Parts Gives Beauty to Composition

Because fruits and vegetables are essentially form, they appeal particularly to the potential sculptor, although the potential painter who enjoys broad splashes of hue finds them equally artful.

There are as many types of fruit-vegetable arrangements as persons to make them, but some general hints in assembling will prove helpful in achieving the three aspects of good design—unity, variety, and vitality.

VARIETY GIVES INTEREST

Be sure each form has reason for inclusion in your design, not used because it happens to be in your larder. Combine forms that in some respect are the same, in others different (Plates 62, 63). Such practice

65

63 OLD WINE *This imaginative arranger explains that "antique bottles were used in combination with gnarled wood and black grapes to suggest a grape arbor. Mellow tones of red and blue helped convey the illusion of flowing wine." Plum branches, dracaena leaves, ivy, blue grapes and deep red anemones comprise the plant material.*
ARRANGER: MRS. WILLIAM GEORGE HUNTER.
PHOTOGRAPHER: BOUTRELLE-SEVECKE

assures harmonious relationship which has a degree of variation that is generally more appealing than uniformity.

For unity within variety, long shapes, such as carrots, cucumbers, or bananas, are linked with round shapes, as beets, turnips, apples. Use more of one shape than the other in respect for the principle of dominance. The lesser quality, by virtue of being different, emphasizes the dominant aspect and thereby enriches design (Plates 64, 65).

62 (Opposite) SEMI-TROPICAL FLAVOR *An inventive arranger has made a container by fastening a wooden chopping bowl on an old balustrade. A coconut in an outer shell is the "character builder" in this group of forms appealing in association. Sameness of rounds holds the design together. Monotony is prevented by variations in hue, value, and chroma A simulated alligator leather glass, heavy pottery plate, natural burlap cloth (washed several times to make it suitable for table use) suggest the complete setting with decoration towards one corner of the table.*
ARRANGER: MRS. A. F. STEUBING.   PHOTOGRAPHER: WHITEHALL STUDIO

64 (Left) NASSAU INFLUENCE *Reminiscent of the beautiful head carriage of street vendors with large fruit-filled baskets, material is here grouped in strong upright pattern in a pottery bowl atop a dark pottery head. Forms at the base bring the composition into visual balance.*
ARRANGER: MRS. GEORGE GOLDSON.
PHOTOGRAPHER: BRAMORE STUDIO

65 (Opposite) TROPICANA *Large, medium, and small contrasting forms and harmonious hues are arranged on a Chinese-red base, high on one side, sweeping low on the other. Gladiolus, Bali bust, and "fans" add to tropical atmosphere. To make the latter, bamboo place mats are folded and wired in shape.*
ARRANGER: MRS. H. C. STATON.
PHOTOGRAPHER: PORTLAND OREGONIAN

In putting them together, arrange shapes to carry the eye easily from one form or group of forms to another by avoiding sudden and sharp contrast. For example, if you start with a dominance of circular forms, re-echo the curves in connecting areas.

RHYTHMIC PROPORTIONS VITAL IN SIZE, HUE, TEXTURE

As to size, hue, and texture, avoid uniformity of equal divisions. Employ a dominance of each element to gain unity or oneness through undivided interest. Character (formal or informal, rugged or refined) is thus established.

An assemblage of large, medium, and small sizes, and of graded hue, value, and tone, gives rhythmic sequence to enable the eye to move easily through the decoration (Plate 66). Rhythmic movement supplies vitality and animation.

COLOR HIGHLIGHTS FORM

Pleasing combination of hue is as important as that of size and shape. You may enjoy color for itself, but in arrangement it is seldom

isolated. Each hue in a combination is a spot of color, so rhythmic relationship is imperative.

For satisfaction, group like hues and tonal values into areas and distribute these to produce a definite appeal. For rich, forceful, striking effect, consider contrasted hues (jacket plate) and values (Plate 67). Plate 68 shows the contrast distributed in a manner to soften the force of attraction. To develop a more subtle charm, use a blend of graded hue and tonal value (Plates 69, 70). When emphasis is on

66 FOR A TABLE ON THE PATIO *In effective contrast of light against dark, and smooth against surface pattern, a pineapple, artichokes, a pomegranate, grapes, pears, limes, acorn squashes, tangerines, and knotty textured gourds are arranged with driftwood in rhythmic gradation.*
ARRANGER: MRS. GEORGE GOLDSON.
PHOTOGRAPHER: BRAMORE STUDIO

67   TIMELESS DESIGN   *In a milk-glass compote a pattern combines high and low values to achieve table decoration that has carrying power making an arrangement effective from a distance. This is an important attribute in banquet-hall decoration.*
ARRANGER: MRS. E. B. HEADDEN.   PHOTOGRAPHER: HORACE SHELDON

68 (Opposite) A FALL SILHOUETTE   *On a black glass cake-stand, a cup pinholder supports viburnum in water. A feeling of lightness is maintained at the top with bright, warm hues massed in the center to produce a lively arrangement, a satisfactory supplementary decoration on the sideboard.*
ARRANGER: MRS. LOUIS H. AMER.   PHOTOGRAPHER: EDWARD MAHER

the warm tones of the red and yellow color families, the plan is warm and informal; blues, purples, greens, and whites give more sophistication and formality, although Plate 45 proves exception to the rule. Another possibility is just one hue with its variations of

69 (Left) HARMONY ON THE TABLE
Laid for a comfortable supper on the porch, rich dark violet-red dahlias and mahogany-red cannas are arranged on a pinholder in one end of a Gypsy soup-bone kettle of iron. Purple eggplant and blue-violet plums add to close harmony of hue for late evening mood. A maroon-textured cloth relates this decoration to white-red patterned dishes. Wise indeed is the homemaker who chooses her background color from a dominant hue in the pattern of her dishes.
ARRANGER: MRS. F. PALMER HART.

PHOTOGRAPHER: BOUTRELLE

70 (Right) BRUNCH ON THE SUN PORCH *becomes a lively cheerful occasion when a wideawake cock, symbol of the morning, lords over an arrangement staged for mid-morning repast. Made of metal, he allies the decoration to the metal table. Fresh okra pods repeat the greenish hue of his feathers; bright red dahlias, green saxifraga leaves, and a second metal rooster complete the grouping at the base of tall bamboo, its vertical line signifying the growth of day.*
ARRANGER: MRS. SAMUEL LASKER.

PHOTOGRAPHER: WILLIAM ALLEN

value and intensity. In such a scheme, grading from dark to light or light to dark directs attention to the most important areas in the design.

Never overlook the advantage of dark and light tones in any ensemble. Contrast supplies carrying power and may add distinction. And a touch of light against dark will prevent a feeling of heaviness in design (Plate 71).

71 SIMPLE COMPOSITION RICH WITH HARVEST SPIRIT *Yellow and red lady apples, red and green grapes, limes, and laurel foliage are arranged on a black antique scale. The accessory weights add sufficient interest to the smaller grouping to compensate for the heavier area to the left of the vertical center axis.*

ARRANGER: MRS. E. B. HEADDEN.   PHOTOGRAPHER: HORACE SHELDON

In general, use forceful contrast (in hue, value, or tone) only in location of particular interest in the pattern, and even then in small masses. But almost always a bright note adds zest. Small areas of intense hue against planes of dull are effective (Plate 72). In Plate 73, limes and green pears indicate this with sensitive consideration for balanced color in a plan of mixed hues. In Plate 33, it is offered in the rose-red of strawberries. Two orange tangerines supply bright accent in Plate 64.

72   "HARVEST TIPS THE SCALES"   *With beauty such as this, it is easy to understand that man appreciated fruit on his dining board even before he did flowers. The arranger's imagination has planned this buffet setting for high color interest—gleaming brass with wheat, corn husks, lemons, and squashes to blend; reds, red-orange, greens, and blues of grapes, apples, Indian corn, persimmons, and oak-tree foliage to contrast. An unpatterned cloth to match the hue of the golden wheat would dramatize the color tones.*
ARRANGER: MRS. GEORGE GOLDSON.   PHOTOGRAPHER: BOUTRELLE-SEVECKE

73 SIMPLE DESIGN WITH GREAT CHARM *Limes, green pears, pome-granates, purple grapes join with budding magnolia branches, dracaena, and galax leaves in a Chinese bronze container. on a chartreuse fabric, exemplifying harmony when forms in some respects are alike, in others quite different.*
ARRANGER: MRS. GEORGE J. HIRSCH. PHOTOGRAPHER: NEW YORK TIMES

VISUAL STABILITY

The quantity of strong and dark hue is a matter of balance, generally observed by bright areas occupying the smallest planes, and the darkest tone low in the design. In other words, for balance, hues that are "forceful" or "heavy" (as is the case with form) are kept low. Heaviness is visual as well as physical. Forms that are dark, or bright, and have "rough" textures appear heavier than those of the same size in light or dull hue and smooth surface. By way of example, red or purple grapes are "heavier" than a cluster of green grapes of the same dimensions.

Plate 52 proves that the practice of "heavy low" is only a rule to be broken if occasion demands. Here the light value of green grapes reaches out and has more attractive pull on the eye than the receding tone surrounding it, and so compensates for lack of physical weight.

CENTER OF INTEREST AIDS PICTORIAL COMPLETENESS

Rely on your knowledge of arranging flowers to establish an adequate interest area in your design pattern (Plate 74). If you study the examples offered in this book, you will find that the more complex

74 A RUMPUS ROOM BUFFET *Opposing lines lend excitement to this design, appropriate in a gay rumpus room. Cohesion is achieved through an interest center where the beak of the natural feathered, red-throated bird meets the beige-colored burrs of the sycamore tree. On a cloth of red corduroy, green leaves of clivia and Chinese evergreen, yellow-spotted green dieffenbachia, and green grapes add the spice of contrast.*

ARRANGER: MRS. MONROE GREENBAUM.   PHOTOGRAPHER: HERBERT STUDIO

75 FREE-STANDING CENTER ARRANGEMENT *This design building
up in the center and spreading low over the edge of the compote shows a center
of interest of soft downy peaches and geranium leaves. On the reverse side the
eye is directed to red-cheeked pears and green grapes at the focal point. All fit
together in harmony of shape, hue, and texture to make an arrangement pleasing
and different from various angles.*
ARRANGER: MRS. H. FULTON MURPHY.   PHOTOGRAPHER: OFFIE LITES

the design, the greater is the need for this magnet of unity to pull the various forms, hues, and textures together into visual oneness. I like to sit down to make a table arrangement; it brings the logical location for emphasis into better focus.

Whether or not attention is brought to an area on the pivot of balance (the central axis) or away from it, attention it demands must be compensated for by distribution of all other units in the design. Unless the whole surface of the composition is visible at one time (is without forceful stopping spots for the eye), unity is sacrificed.

If your decoration occupies the center position on the table, make it pleasing from all angles. To increase engaging design, arrange the center of interest area on different sides with some variation. In a bowl or compote, build up the design to a moderate height at the center, and let the material droop over the sides, and it will be pleasing all around (Plate 75).

SIZE OF DECORATIVE UNIT ON THE TABLE

There is no rule as to the size of the decorative unit on the table. Be guided by convenience, efficiency, and eye appeal. The important thing, let there be no crowding. Remember, decoration is but a part of the all-over setting.

In many fruit-vegetable plans, the main axis around which attraction is equalized is horizontal rather than vertical as in a floral arrangement; so the height of the plant material can be equal to that of the container without violating good proportion. Constant experimentation reveals many possibilities, but I emphasize advisability to guard against a too-flat grouping when fruits and/or vegetables are arranged on a tray or plaque. Adjust them to carry the eye away from the flat table surface to break the monotony of too much sameness (Plates 16, 41), or include something for a definite upward swing (Plates 32, 66).

Height, of course, must not be a detriment to comfort. The too-high center arrangement may interfere with a view of those seated opposite. At the end of the table or against the wall, the sky can be the limit of height (Plate 76)!

76 (Opposite) NOVELTY ON THE SIDE TABLE   *On a walnut silverware chest, two Cuban pineapples are garlanded with sunshine-yellow flower heads threaded together in Hawaiian lei style. Height is gained in slender spears of gladiolus foliage. Bosc pears and pineapples carry the tone of the chest; peppers and avocados, the foliage green. In texture the shiny fruits repeat the sheen of the polished chest and aid harmony, to which all qualities should contribute.*
ARRANGER: MRS. CLIFFORD E. CYPHERS.   PHOTOGRAPHER: CHARLES F. CYPHERS

CANDLES—CORRECT USE FOR HEIGHT AND LIGHT

Candles are ideal as uplifting lines, but regard their use with thought. Except for the novelty type, which are dominantly decorative rather than utilitarian (Plate 88), or those employed for symbolism (Plate 4), use candles only when there is need for illumination.

Some hues are beautiful in sunshine, but completely lost under artificial light (unless it approximates the light of day). Pale yellow becomes almost white; blue and violet are neutralized almost to gray. On the other hand, red and orange are enriched under yellow light, so they are useful to "pep up" weakened hues.

HEIGHT BY OTHER MEANS

If candle function is not desired, achieve vertical uplift by other means—a figurine, perhaps. Or gain it with groupings on different levels—one on a pedestal of a sort, or in an elevated container, arranged to bring the eye down to a group at the base (Plate 22).

Long-stemmed flowers and tall foliage or branches (bare or in flower or leaf) are usable. Plates 29 and 51 are interesting examples.

COMBINING FLOWERS AND FOLIAGE WITH FRUITS AND VEGETABLES

To combine with fruits and vegetables, select flowers and foliage with an eye to hue, form, and texture relationship. If they are employed as garnish (Plate 15) rather than for height (Plate 31), keep them fresh in small vials of water or in water-filled "blow up" balloons fastened with rubber bands about the inserted stems. Either of these is easy to conceal among the forms. Or if flowers and leaves have been conditioned by deep water soaking, simply wrap the stem ends in wet cotton, then wrap with waxed paper. I have kept foliage fresh by inserting the stem in a grape or citrus fruit in the decoration. I recall with pleasure once using a segment of watermelon in which the inserted stems remained perky and fresh.

When combining flowers and/or foliage with fruits and/or vegetables, allow one classification to dominate. If your desire is an arrangement with the accent on the flowers, for example, be sure that the set forms and bright hues of the fruit do not overpower the more delicate blooms. On the other hand, if flowers or foliage are but to garnish the arrangement, let the fruit dominate.

Autumn-toned tree leaves, galax, ivy, begonia are among varieties that serve well as effective adornment, but use them with purpose. Don't fill every little crevice. Employ only enough to intensify beauty, not so many as to destroy it. Select them to blend color tones, or to emphasize or contrast hue, depending on your intent.

THE MECHANICS OF AN ARRANGEMENT

Fasten a large form, such as squash, eggplant, or pineapple, securely to the container or base. Control the placement with floral clay or by setting it in a curtain ring foundation. A pin-holder is usable for anchorage, although it injures and hastens decay.

Other forms are secured with small brads pushed into juxtaposed fruits or vegetables. A hard-shelled gourd may require an inserted small screw eye to slip over the exposed end of a brad in a softer neighboring form. Toothpicks (I like the firm plastic picks) will do for small forms. Small wire hairpins serve to hold grapes in place.

When you want material to fall gracefully over the edge of a bowl or compote, as in Plates 8 and 20, place a lightweight stick across the opening, and secure the fruit to the ends with fine wire or florists' thread in such a way that control is not in evidence in the completed arrangement.

To secure high placement, impale forms on false stems. Twigs are usable, but knitting needles are easier to insert into firm, hard models (Plates 59, 64).

Support short bits of vine as, in Plate 77, with cup hooks, which are easily concealed in near-by shapes. The wire hairpin, too, will serve in this capacity.

If your supply of material is limited, be not dismayed. Props of crumpled paper, crushed chicken wire, even an inverted bowl can serve as "filler" under the fruits. By such means, a little material can be made to look like a lot. Plate 75 might well exemplify such construction.

TEN QUESTIONS YOU MIGHT ASK

In any single book on arrangements, the scope of subject coverage is necessarily limited. Here I can present only an idea of technique, restriction, and possibility. It is probable that additional questions concerning decorating the dining table with fruits and/or vegetables have come to mind. Perhaps your special problem is discussed in the answers to the following questions selected from those repeatedly asked.

1. *Is a white cloth ever effective with fruits or vegetables?*

Indeed, yes. Actually the large expanse of white tends to diminish the strength of bright hues, when this is desired, and makes light values pure and vigorous.

2. *Where is the best location for the decorative unit?*

Any place where it conforms to seating arrangement without crowding. A decoration is a failure if it interferes with service or cannot be seen at all.

3. *Must a decoration at center placement be symmetrical?*

To harmonize with already established uniformity in place settings, maintain a feeling of symmetry in the centerpiece, but avoid monotony through intelligent variety within the decoration (Plate 75).

4. *What is the best shape for the decoration?*

In general, let your decoration follow the lines of the table. A round arrangement will break the rhythm of a long, rectangular board. If a bowl is right in texture and hue, but too round in shape, arrange the material to flow horizontally from it to achieve an elongated pattern. An oval theme is pleasing on a round table; its curvilinear pattern is harmonious with dish and glass shapes, yet its elongated contour supplies variety.

5. *How can flowers at one end of the table and fruit at the other be harmonized?*

Such a plan (or fruit grouped at the base of flowers) can be tied together through texture and color.

6. *Why are formal settings more difficult to do well than informal?*

The formal pattern is restricted to certain traditions with the net result that it is often "too conventional" or "too ornate" without intrinsic beauty.

77 HANDSOME SIMPLICITY *White and gold monogrammed china and stemmed goblets contribute to traditional elegance when formality is desired. The rayon damask cloth is particularly attractive because of its lustrous shimmer. A beautiful brass and marble scale is an authentic copy of one used in the 1800's. Candles are matched to the cloth or fruit as the hostess desires. This suggested setting will reflect a diversity of moods simply by a change of hue in the background cloth.*

ARRANGER: MRS. H. HENRY STALEY. PHOTOGRAPHER: SCATTERGOOD STUDIO

7. *How many candles should be used, and what height and hue are best?*

Many tables are spoiled by the choice of candles. In color have them match exactly the dominant hue in the decoration, or a subdued tone, or a subordinate hue in the color scheme.

White or ivory tapers, rather than modern colored candles, seem more harmonious with antique holders, which were designed by silversmiths for the mellow-toned candles of yesteryear (Plate 78).

For the comfort of your family and guests, let the candles be tall or short, but never at a height at which their flame would annoy the eyes of those seated at the table. Tall candles in low holders, and short in tall candlesticks are more pleasing aesthetically than short in low, and long in tall. If there is no other illumination, at least four candles are required to light the average dining table evenly, but don't restrict their use to the table. On the buffet and server they will contribute light and charm.

8. *Is there any choice for the style or type of table?*

Setting the table is a personal problem, its style depending on the tastes of family and guests, the occasion for which it is planned, and the type of entertainment desired—formal or informal, to accommodate a limited number of seated diners or an unlimited number served in buffet manner.

You might feature a coming holiday by using color and symbols appropriate to the day and by introducing a humorous note, perhaps, to amuse your most intimate friends or children. Novelty decoration has its place, but for general use all around the year, nothing surpasses flowers, fruits, and vegetables.

9. *How does the home table differ from that in show competition?*

In competition, a table is a distinct unit; at home, it is only a part of a whole. Walls, rugs, draperies, upholstery are considered for color and character agreement when setting the home table.

Without question, color goes far toward harmonizing. It is helpful to let one hue (selected from the dishes, cloth, or background of the room) run through the entire setting.

10. *Is there any standard of judgment against which a table can be compared?*

To analyze tables against an ideal of perfection, flower show judges use a scale of points devised for the particular entries to be considered. A recommended scale of perfection is as follows:

Appropriateness to occasion (in the home) or to schedule (in the show)	20
Suitability of combination of all materials	20
Completeness and correctness of service	20
Perfection of decorative unit	15
Distinction and originality	15
Condition (neatness and freshness)	10
	100

APPROPRIATENESS TO OCCASION

When you set a table, you are indicating the type and time of day for which the meal is planned. To classify generally, tables are divided into breakfast, luncheon, dinner, and supper settings for seated or buffet service.

Breakfast is an informal affair, and a bright and gay mood is expected. Pottery and colored tumblers fit the mode of bright color and coarsely woven mats, runners, doilies, or cloth. The color contrast provided by checks or plaids is appropriately stimulating.

78   TEA-TIME DECOR   *Cherished items from the past—old pink lustre china, Sheffield silver candlesticks, hand-drawn lace cloth—produce a contemporary fireside table with nostalgic appeal. Strawberries, lady and small red apples, green-white grapes, and acacia foliage fill a three-tier china container in pyramidal pattern having its prototype in an early way with table fruits.*
ARRANGER: MRS. SIMEON TAYLOR SHIELDS.
PHOTOGRAPHER: MRS. C. COLTON TUTTLE

79 FOR TASTE AND EYE APPEAL *Often the table itself, as with this teak-
wood, inspires appropriate appointments and decoration. For this dessert course,
old Chinese pewter dishes, teapot and caddy, the thousand-eye cups and saucers,
and Cloisonné plate harmonize. Soft gray tones dominantly carried around the
table and repeated in the center pewter container are complimentary to varied
hues in the fruits. When fruits are eaten, Chinese evergreen remains in a three-
dimensional pattern of "living line", appreciated by the Chinese in recognition of
the spaciousness of Nature which influences their art.*
ARRANGER: MRS. LAMBERT D. LE MAIRE.   PHOTOGRAPHER: A. L. KNOWLTON-SCHEN

The luncheon hour is "the pause that refreshes," so colorful linen is somewhat subdued. White too is adaptable. Select mats, runners, doilies (oblong or the newer round shapes placed to hang partly over the table's edge), or cloth in white, natural, or pastel finely woven linen, embroidered linen, or lace. With natural linen, use napkins to match; with pastels, have them match or contrast in hue. Footed tumblers or short-stemmed goblets are proper, depending on the degree of formality you desire; the latter have more dignity than the former.

Reserve damask for the evening meal, for its heavy distinction invites relaxed and leisurely dining well-timed at the day's end. Only damask napkins are right with such a cloth. Porcelain china and long-stemmed crystal goblets add to the formal atmosphere.

Subdued color is satisfactory on the family evening-hour table or on one set informally for a friendly gathering at dinner. The choice of an all-over cloth or individual place covers is a personal one. You may prefer the former to the cut-up pattern given to a table surface by mats or doilies, which may distract somewhat from the restful tone of an evening table. On the other hand, you may delight in exposing the polished table wood and deliberately select mats or doilies as the homemaker did in Plate 79. Today, under relaxed traditional dictates, the option is entirely yours.

The American institution, the buffet meal, and a table set for supper on a restful Sunday or holiday are always informal and are either rustic in mood with bright hues, coarse weaves, pottery, and sturdy glassware or elegant with fine linen, china, and crystal.

In the show, interpret "appropriateness to schedule" to mean how well the table conforms to the requirements set forth in the classification. By way of example, Plate 72 would rate high in fulfillment of demands in the class title "Harvest Tips the Scales." Very much to the point are Plates 41, 43, and 66 to carry out such a schedule classification as a "Table Set for Outdoor Dining."

SUITABILITY OF COMBINATION OF MATERIALS

In the second designated quality in the point scale, consider color, texture, shape, and size relationships of all that is on the table. In color analysis, let hues blend or contrast with a dominant or key hue running through the whole. Have textures comfortably balanced, using "rough" with "rough" and "fine" with "fine," but with attention to fitting variety. Repeat shapes for the sake of unity, again supplying variation to prevent monotony of too much repetition. As to scale or size relationship, don't overlook the decorative unit as a whole in relation to the size of the table; a too-large decoration will contribute to a crowded and untidy appearance, while a too-small unit will be dwarfed to insignificance and be meaningless.

COMPLETENESS AND CORRECTNESS OF SERVICE

The third quality compels your attention to the demands of tradition, social usage, practicality, and functionalism—in short, to table etiquette. By way of example, unmatched dishes (provided they relate in character as in Plate 15) are acceptable and advisable on the informal table, but not on the strictly formal. According to traditional custom, all dishes appearing at one time on this type of setting are matched, although dishes of one course may differ from those of another.

A triumph of good table setting is functionalism or ease and comfort of service. Allow at least two feet of space for each person seated, with service plate and flatware neatly lined up about one inch from the table edge. Arrange your dining buffet for a practical aspect in self-service by your guests. In every case, avoid an overfilled and crowded table and one too sparse and appearing empty of food.

PERFECTION OF DECORATIVE UNIT

The fourth quality refers to the decoration as a distinct unit. Here you take into account its assemblage based on the fundamental principles of art that underscore any artistic arrangement.

DISTINCTION AND ORIGINALITY

Next in the judging scale, you must consider distinction and originality. A table correctly laid and fittingly decorated will satisfy your aesthetic sense, but if you allow your ingenuity and imaginative faculty to keep pace with your selective ability, you can produce something of lasting interest for those who see it. Plates 74, 76, and

100 show how planned novelty can give an original touch to lift a setting out of the ordinary.

CONDITION—NEATNESS AND FRESHNESS

The last quality has to do with the neatness of the whole. Flower show judges expect to find flowers and foliage well hardened to remain fresh and perky throughout the show hours. Fresh fruits and vegetables must be exactly that—fresh! And, clean! Dried material must be free of broken stems and raggedy torn leaves or pods and should show no trace of mold or dust.

Well-pressed linen rates over that which shows the muss of handling. Glasses must be sparkling and free from finger smudge. Each plate must be placed carefully with monogram or scene facing the diner, and each cup with the handle facing *evenly* to his right. Candles should be firm and straight in their holders.

5

TABLE DECORATION

THROUGHOUT THE YEAR

Unlimited Scope for Holiday and Commemorative Themes and Ideas

THANKSGIVING IN THE HARVEST MONTH

Fruits and vegetables are synonymous with Thanksgiving. Throughout the years, they have been a part of harvest festivals celebrated with merriment and feasting.

In temperate zones, apples, pumpkins, carrots, squashes, peppers, and corn are among the traditional field and garden material. In the

80 PEACE AND PLENTY *The grape is marketed throughout our country, so its symbolism of fruitfulness and good cheer fits it to Thanksgiving decoration anywhere in our land. The Pioneer Woman and Boy in bronze against old wood sets the theme. Wheat, representative of the staff of life, gives height and silhouette to this third-dimensional pattern. A forward rhythm adds impetus to this moving composition.*
ARRANGER: MISS MARGARET D. GRUMBINE.   PHOTOGRAPHER: BOUTRELLE

Boutrelle · Sevecke
NEW YORK

South, pomegranates and Chinese persimmons are grown profusely. And at the market everywhere is a copious supply from which to choose. Whatever your source, resist the temptation to select "some of each," for too great a variety makes harmonious combination difficult.

Whether you favor extreme restraint or elaborate extravagance in decoration, work toward simplicity of design. In any pattern, a well-ordered plan achieves this goal. The result is a more forceful expression, even of the abundance that is typical of Thanksgiving, than is possible with a hodgepodge of form and hue (Plates 80 through 84).

82 (Above) DISTRIBUTION IS SO IMPORTANT *In contrast to symmetrical balance achieved with a pair of like containers in plate 34, two alike or varied ones, as here, can be balanced asymmetrically to effect one distinct unit. Placement of chrysanthemums carries the eye to a point from which it swings downward into the heart of the composition, thereby attaining pictorial completeness. Fruits and vegetables add body to stabilize the shallow bowls.*
ARRANGER: MRS. DUNHAM C. JONES.   PHOTOGRAPHER: BOUTRELLE-SEVECKE

81 (Opposite) BIG SCALE HARVEST *Symmetry directs attention to the Buddha as center of interest in this lavish design. Simplicity reigns, for such quality is acquired not through a minimum of material necessarily, but by direct and forceful expression with a little or a lot. Of original charm is the giant Hubbard squash halved to expose its orange-yellow meat and holding symbols of Thanksgiving at the feet of the Chinese god. A pineapple halved in like manner is lovely with grapes.*
ARRANGER: MRS. GEORGE GOLDSON.   PHOTOGRAPHER: BOUTRELLE

83 (Above) HIGH-COLOR STYLING   *On a tangerine cloth, pottery plates with fruit wreath pattern harmonize with black and green grapes, avocados, and peppers, rust-hued pears, kumquats, limes, and a satin-skinned persimmon. The most is made of the latter—note the flower calyx which it wears like a crown. Chartreuse of napkins and candles in wrought iron holders contributes drama and beauty to the character of this modern Thanksgiving table.*
ARRANGERS: MRS. WILLIAM WHEELER; MRS. DUNHAM C. JONES.
PHOTOGRAPHER: BOUTRELLE-SEVECKE

84 (Right) TRIBUTE TO RURAL HARVEST   *is this combination of dried and fresh fall bounty. Note the ingenious conversion of a cutlery box from America's past into a "modern" container by attaching cupboard clothes hook legs. Mellow tones in the aged wood bring out the color and detail in corn stalk and tassel, variegated corn, grains, squashes, grapes, pears, black walnuts, and gourds. Overall color in plant material is tan and green with contrast of red tones.*
ARRANGER: MRS. JOHN H. SQUIRES, JR.   PHOTOGRAPHER: BOUTRELLE-SEVECKE

CHRISTMAS AT YEAR'S END

Christmas is as radiant and bright as a star and as full of faith as a tiny seed fulfilling its mission to humanity. In decoration, spiritual quality is often sacrificed to novel, sometimes garish, ornamentation. Gaiety is desired, yes, but not to suppress religious significance.

They cannot be eaten, but fruits and vegetables brushed with silver or gold as described on page 59 have a radiant quality. Combined with natural reds, symbolic of joy, blues and purples of peace, and greens of eternal life, the inner meaning of Christmas is conveyed.

WREATHS AND GARLANDS IN DELLA ROBBIA STYLE

The ancients attached fruits, nuts, and flowers to garlands, but it is the ceramic wreaths framing the Madonna and Babe against a blue background that typify Christmas spirit. This style popularized by the Della Robbia artists of the Renaissance is adaptable to effective table decoration (Plate 5), and the wreaths are not difficult to make.

Small fruits, as limes, lemons, lady apples, kumquats, and cranberries, are among the most satisfactory in the table garland. To make ready for attachment to a green foundation wreath, purchased from the florist or made by the homemaker herself, impale cranberries on toothpicks, and wire them together in bunches of three (more in a cluster is difficult to handle). Prepare other forms individually by pushing a length of wire (long enough to fasten the fruit on the foundation) through the centers, twisting the ends behind and close to the fruit.

Shellac the wired forms, not only to seal puncture wounds and thereby lessen speed of decay (they will last from two to three weeks), but to add luster to simulate the enameled porcelains of the Della Robbia artists. Use a brush to apply shellac, as dipping imparts an unattractive coating. Don't be tempted to use a "quick spray" varnish for it contains a chemical that blackens the fruit.

When dry, attach the forms to the wreath by pushing the wires through to the back and twisting them for anchorage. Fasten them securely for ease in handling when the table is cleared between meals.

Heighten the porcelainlike texture by adding shiny leaves with each group of fruits and nuts. (Nuts are wired as described on page 56.)

The leaves of magnolia grandiflora are especially lovely. Incidentally, unripened fruits (selected to last) gradually color under the artificial glaze.

Plate 85 represents a contemporary adaptation of the Della Robbia style.

85   THE SYMBOLIC WREATH   *To make this emblem of remembrance, chartreuse satin ribbon was wound around a three-inch frame. Groupings of kumquats, lady apples, and holly leaves were sewed to this foundation.*
ARRANGER: MRS. FREDERICK W. LEWIS.   PHOTOGRAPHER: BOUTRELLE-SEVECKE

FROSTED FRUITS

A "frosted fruit" variation is irresistible. Frosted grapes are pictured in Plate 61, but any fruit can be so treated. To prepare them, first wash them and dry thoroughly. Dip each piece into frothy beaten egg white, then into granulated sugar. Dry on waxed paper. Arrange in a pleasing pattern on a wreath of green.

This translucent sparkle disguise does not preserve as does shellac, but unlike shellacked fruit, the sugar-coated can be eaten. To revive an old custom, arrange them in a Wedgwood compote, or lacking this coveted possession, in any beautiful container of china, glass, or silver. Tables of the eighteenth century held such "taste treat" decoration for the dessert course; we too will enjoy the delectable flavor of frosted fruit.

A CHRISTMAS WINDOW AND THE SMALL TREE

On Christmas morning, push your breakfast table against the window for fresh enchantment. On it arrange a group of highly polished red apples adorned with holly. Use no other decoration except a sprig or two of berry-laden holly between the glass of your regular window and that of the temporary storm sash. You'll be amazed at this easy-to-do and simple beauty. Between the two panes of glass, the holly remains fresh and lovely until, on Twelfth-night (January 6), tradition dictates removal of all holiday decoration. It will be with reluctance that you banish this spot of cheer.

Many stories surround the Christmas tree. If you plan one for table or sideboard, a legend told in the Holy Land is suggestive. Three trees, it is related, wished to offer gifts to the little Prince of Peace. The Olive and Palm gave generously of their fruits, but the Evergreen had none. It stretched its arms to heaven for help. In answer, stars descended to nestle in the uplifted boughs. One remained on the topmost branch; many others turned into beautiful fruits. Ever since, Christmas trees are trimmed with fruits and glistening stars.

86   A TREE OF LIFE   *On a homemade frame, carefully selected artificial fruits (fresh forms could be substituted) and glossy fresh magnolia leaves are wired to blend from purple at the base to light reds and yellows at the top. Vigil candles in green glass holders are attached on the ends of the espaliered "limbs". Such a tree is addition to any space in need of a bright touch, particularly handsome against the wall rising from the mantel shelf. To give it slip-proof security, let its "trunk" rest in a rubber furniture leg cup or on a piece of sponge rubber.*
ARRANGER AND PHOTOGRAPHER: MRS. H. S. STATON

Try an all-over pattern of lady apples in groups of three to symbolize the Trinity. Or in the manner of a Byzantine cone motif, spiral a "ribbon of fruit" from top to bottom. Or try an espaliered tree for Christmas charm (Plate 86).

OTHER CHRISTMAS THEMES

Plate 87 illustrates a novel and decorative idea for gift presentation. Throughout the book you will find many arrangements suited to Christmas arrangement. Among them, Plates 3, 4, 9, 17, 18, 19, and 22 give suggestions for varied ideas and locations in the home.

JOYOUS SYMBOLS FOR THE NEW YEAR

Across the nation, people attempt to express life's ideal of transmitting good traits from the past to the future in New Year celebration. In decoration, there is no substitute for a cornucopia (horn of plenty) overflowing with colorful fruits and/or vegetables given us by the year just ended. It matches a mood of expectation, for the seeds of each hold promise of glorious, beneficial things to come. A bit of seaweed included is appropriate for its ancient symbolism of "The Eternal." A pomander ball made to impart a spicy fragrance in your linen closet (page 62) can be decoratively used among the fruits as a symbol of time.

Holiday Flower Arrangements * suggests the following: "In the spirit of gaiety, let your decoration gleam, glitter, and shine even brighter than on Christmas, for New Year's Day is a final fling to the exhilarant mood." In this practice, the New Year horn of plenty is distinguished from that of Thanksgiving. If you enjoy symbolism, include a shiny bell or two, but any sparkling touch is appropriate.

For something novel and attractive, add various-sized transparent glass bubbles to a grouping of the more refined and delicate fruits and/or vegetables. (They are too dainty in character for the "coarse" varieties.) These are sold to beautify the home aquarium, but bubbles, you know, are full of promise! Whatever bright touches you include, be sure you group them with meaning; to scatter causes design confusion.

After New Year gaiety, life has settled to a stable key. Rush of holiday preparation is gone, and so is the content of our purse! Spending has been fun, but life's demands require that pockets bulge again. Toward this, fruits and vegetables help in playing a double role. Today they are decoration to feed the eye; tomorrow, salad or soup to feed the body.

* Published by Hearthside Press Inc., New York, 1954.

87 A GIFT BASKET *Candy, fruit, a plant, and red and green cellophane-wrapped gifts fill a gift basket. "Almond ribbon" covering the handle is made with almonds attached to Scotch tape. Almond "grapes" can be made as described on page 56. Packages of hard candy on the bottom of the basket elevate the arrangement of long-needled pine, red grapes, and small red and yellow apples.*

ARRANGER: MRS. EARL MILES.   PHOTOGRAPHER: BOUTRELLE-SEVECKE

88 ROMANTIC LUNCHEON TABLE *Blending old and new, a graceful Hogarth curve of berried branches, roses, and small fruits is arranged in an antique pink overlay container hung with cut prisms. The cut glass wine-filled decanter holds the friendly "cup that cheers". Sculptured silverware pattern complements smooth pink-and-gold handpainted plates by Sacha Brastoff. These and goblets of smoky-pink glass add truly modern distinction. Heart-shaped candles key the table to a sentimental mood for a valentine or engagement party; Staffordshire ceramic flower place-card holders and sheer Chinese embroidered linen laid over a pink liner add color.*
ARRANGER: MRS. ALFRED S. GRUSSNER.   PHOTOGRAPHER: A. L. KNOWLTON-SCHEN

SYMBOLS OF LOVE AND PATRIOTISM FOR FEBRUARY

February, the shortest month, has more "special" days than any other month, and each offers opportunity for imaginative decoration. You can go romantic in February; be frivolous to honor St. Valentine (Plate 88). Symbols of love in vegetables and fruits can make your decoration a "conversation piece." In legend we learn that if a lass places a pod of nine peas on her doorstep, she will wed the first young man to cross it. The cucumber, in some countries, is a token of romance. The origin of the pear as the heart's emblem is lost in antiquity.

Or let a more austere sentiment pay tribute to two great Americans whose births we celebrate. In a patriotic plan, use lots of red—plump red apples, or luscious red cherries, perhaps. Combined decorously with evergreens, symbolic of strength and endurance, American ideals stand revealed. A red and green plan is shown in Plate 89.

MARCH BRINGS THE BIRTH OF SPRING
AND ST. PATRICK'S DAY

In autumn Nature reached the ebb of her growing season, but ripened fruits and vegetables were not an end to life. Seeds were scattered to a new beginning. And so, in the month which brings the birth of spring, fruit-vegetable decoration has great appeal. Then too, it is practical, a boon to arrangers in sections of the country still in winter's hold, for garden material is a rarity.

Use the national color of Ireland in tune with St. Patrick and Irish caprice. Green, in arrangement, is not confined to foliage. There are artichokes, cabbages, peppers, cucumbers, grapes, avocados, sprouts, limes, squashes, beans, peas, asparagus, chard, spinach, lettuce, gooseberries, apples, unripe fruits. You will think of others.

Tradition gives us potatoes too—large, well-scrubbed Irish potatoes arranged alone or with flowers and/or foliage.

89　FOR AN INFORMAL COCKTAIL PARTY *With red as the key color, this buffet decoration to be set against a wall is stimulating to winter spirits. The bottle of ruby-red clear glass supports podocarpus foliage with bright red carnations in sizes from bloom to bud. A shallow basket tray holding red and green grapes lightens the whole against a chic dark red cloth. Clear cocktail glasses, shaker, plates and supplementary bowls for cocktail fixings would add sparkle under the light of burning candles in low glass holders.*

ARRANGER: MRS. C. C. THACH.
PHOTOGRAPHER: BOUTRELLE

EASTER ON THE WINGS OF MARCH

For those who appreciate ideas, here is something new, yet ever old—
fruit-vegetable decoration on the Easter table. It is new in that flowers
generally take precedent at this season; it is old in its religious significance of life rejuvenation.

Because it is Easter or simply Spring, it's fun to free your imagination! Keep your arrangements lighthearted and gay with dainty shapes
and delicate hues, for Easter is a joyous day following the solemn
Lenten season. Traditional symbols—birds, bunnies, chicks—are pleasing with them. Eggs, dyed or as Nature intended them, are an amusing addition especially to adornment for the breakfast meal, although
they are appropriate on any Easter table (Plate 90).

90 SET FOR A FRIENDLY FOURSOME *This entertaining-wise hostess
has emphasized Easter hues in snapdragons, lemons, and leaves of the beautiful
red-purple cabbage, and in linen handwoven of silk and non-tarnishable golden
threads. Note the repetition of pattern (for harmony) in silverware handle and
plate design, in triangular arrangement and candle placement; in crossed dolphin
container standard and candelabra arms. The decorative accessory and candy cups
are hand-decorated antique blown eggshells.*
ARRANGERS: MRS. JOSEPH CORTESI; MRS. ALFRED S. GRUSSNER.
PHOTOGRAPHER: A. L. KNOWLTON-SCHEN

APRIL AND MAY WANT COLOR BUT MINIMUM MATERIAL

Spring is the youth of the year; gay and happy color is intimated. To compliment the season, you need only imagination and ingenuity. For example, cover your table with a cloth of green to give an illusion of coolness. Keep your centerpiece simple with green and white in glass to spark your table with refreshing hue.

Or emphasize yellow, the sunshine hue, to signify the sun's nearing rays which cause plant life everywhere to burst open in response. Green is an appropriate accompaniment (Plate 91).

There is still the wonderment of life. Each growing thing seems all-important. Impart this individuality to fruits and vegetables by using a minimum. A few limes, a small grapefruit will supply gradation in size. A cucumber will add shape and hue variance. Asparagus, for all the world like flower buds of grape hyacinth, gives height and goes far to interpret the tone of spring. If you like red, radishes or strawberries add spice, but use its strength with reserve in the spring picture. Plate 92 is novel and pertinent.

Reed baskets, glass containers, white or pastel china fit the delicate character. A light hue in linen is pleasing, but nothing is better than white to enliven light values in an arrangement.

JUNE WITH FRUITS AND VEGETABLES

In the passage of time, June, the month of brides, will bring for some young couples a fourth wedding anniversary, which is symbolized by "fruit and flowers." Luxury decoration in the spirit of the old Flemish and Dutch floral paintings (Plate 5) belongs particularly to this event. In spite of many examples left to us by this school of baroque art, arrangers often neglect this style. What a pity, for just as full orchestration is a symphony in sound compared to a few instruments, so the lavish mixed bunch is a symphony in color compared to a design composed of a minimum of material.

Because this type of arrangement is relatively large, it is in proper placement on the buffet table at the back, or when the table has one end pushed against a wall, in position here with suitable figurines or candles balancing at the other. Its drama is suited also to supplementary decoration on the sideboard where height need not be considered, except in pleasing relationship with the furniture piece itself and the wall space it is to occupy.

SIMPLE AND COOLING DECORATION
IN JULY AND AUGUST

Easy does it on hot, torrid summer days. The simplest meal becomes a party when you serve it outdoors. Fruits and vegetables are practical, for their "heavy" forms do not shift in the breeze (Plates 41, 50).

An all green and white arrangement, as in Plate 2, is particularly pleasing during the dog days of August. The color is cooling in effect, and symbolically is attributed to Ceres, the Roman goddess who presides over the eighth month of the year.

The one fruit or vegetable theme is especially nice at this time when you want a big effect for little effort. Or trim a pineapple for novelty. Well-hardened flower heads or berries, now beginning to color in the garden, are attractive spread through the fruit's green topping.

THE SEPTEMBER PICTURE

Labor Day mealtime is decorated with "fruits of our labor." The day is one of rest, but father won't consider it labor if you ask him to gather his choicest garden products to display in decoration. Just a handful of curved beans, a few smooth pods of peas, an onion or two, a few baby potatoes are all you need for a "quickie" design.

Summer's full-blown beauty is going to seed. Though Indian Summer is not yet with us, its theme is in our minds, so it is logical to reflect it in September table decoration (Plate 28). 'An Indian basket is appropriate for garden products being harvested now. Edible plants from the wild combine well with them—for instance, cattails from

91 (Opposite) AN EASTER IMPRESSION *The golden warmth of sunshine has been likened to the kiss that awakens plant life. Perhaps this symbolism is responsible for the refreshing concept in this Easter breakfast composition. A quaint old wooden cart raises yellow narcissus blooms high, to signify faith and growth. Egg-shaped lemons complete the symbolic response, for Eástere, Saxon goddess of Nature's resurrection, hatched from a golden egg. The hue of oranges echos the cups of flowers combined with greens in a bright and vibrant color plan.* ARRANGER: MRS. JAMES L. FINCH.   PHOTOGRAPHER: BOUTRELLE

the marsh. Indians cherished a meal ground from the rootstock of cattails; early settlers in Virginia pealed the fruiting spikes and enjoyed them roasted. Velvety red sumac from the roadside, cherished by country folks as a substitute for lemon flavor, is just the thing to pick up the red of beets or apples. (Only the gray or white berried sumac is poisonous.)

IN OCTOBER IT'S HALLOWEEN

October is climaxed with merrymaking for the young and young-in-heart. If ever there was a time for novelty decoration, it is now. Plate 59 is suggestive of "comedy" and "terror" masquerade worn as protection against evil spirits that are about on the eve of All Souls' Day. Plates 93 and 94 illustrate imaginative faculty.

And of course, we welcome an old friend—whimsical Jack-o'-lantern, shining with bogus light to lure the unsuspecting. Plate 39 shows the pumpkin used for its beauty alone.

As part of your Halloween decoration, use fat tangy apples and nuts to satisfy frost-snapped appetites (Plate 94). Such a plan seems a part of Halloween, since bobbing for apples, a custom from the Roman Festival of Pomona, goddess of orchards, and roasting of nuts, an old Irish rite, have become tradition.

92 (Opposite) NEW IDEAS ARE ALWAYS WELCOME *Fruit on the wall looks fresh and pleasant when in keeping with other décor. A fisherman's creel filled with strawberry "whoppers" makes a decorative pin-up unit to complement a butter tub of flowering fruit-tree branches. Surely this was inspired by Izaak Walton's tribute to the luscious fruit: "Doubtless God could have made a better berry, but doubtless God never did."*
ARRANGER: MRS. C. C. THACH.   PHOTOGRAPHER: BOUTRELLE

6

THOSE SPECIAL OCCASIONS

Thoughtfulness, Surprise, and Ideas are Elements to be Worked into Special Occasion Decoration

At any meal, on any day, for any occasion, surprise is the goal—salad surprise, dessert surprise, decoration surprise. Fruits and vegetables will always serve the latter well if you combine them with the aid of imagination, an eye that *sees*, and a hand with "know-how." Plates 79, 94, and 95 are among those illustrations which deserve special analysis in this regard. Plate 96 combines plant material and an accessory appropriate to a going-away party buffet. Plate 97 gives attention to the special decorating problem for the unexpected cellar party; Plate 98 illustrates a design for an impromptu breakfast. For that hard-to-decorate narrow space, Plate 99 is a pleasing suggestion.

110

93   UNEXPECTEDNESS FOR NOVEL DECORATION   A *monkey man handcarved in Guam looks wide-eyed at merrymakers about a table decorated with this amusing bit of fancy. The cloth is of russet-orange. Colored glassware, and simple shapes of unpatterned modern pottery echo dark blue hue in the bloom. Napkins of brown tie in with the pineapple, coconut, and fiber matting from the palm tree on which the arrangement rests.*
ARRANGER: MRS. RICHARD WARNER.   PHOTOGRAPHER: BOUTRELLE-SEVECKE

THE MEALTIME TRAY

There is much to do when illness strikes, but attention to the mealtime tray is worth the extra time required. Do it gaily and cleverly to bring a smile to weary lips and a boost to morale and a jaded appetite.

An amusing fruit or vegetable "character" is well worth while. Use toothpicks to fasten a small potato head, crowned with parsley hair, to a parsnip body with carrot legs and arms. Once you begin to make it, original ideas will come to mind.

Try a small "colonial bouquet" displayed on an individual fluted pie tin. Make it with a mound of tiny pickling onions framed with watercress or parsley. Or make a corsage of peas, in and out of pods, yellow beans, a Brussels sprout or two. Attach wire "stems," and wrap them together with florists' parofilm. Use the rim of a small glass or vase to support the corsage upright on the tray.

94 "WHEN GOOD FELLOWS GET
TOGETHER" *Sandwiches on the bird's-eye
wooden plates, beer in the chilled Mettlach
dispenser and steins, figure, and plant material
present eye appeal plus! The decoration has
dual personality achieved with berried shrub
branches, aspidistra and galax leaves, bananas
to carry the line to radishes at the focal area
and wooden leaf which holds shiny red apples
and giant California walnuts to finish off the
snack. When these are eaten, the arrangement
is left intact; the beautifully carved tray main-
tains balance.*

ARRANGER: MRS. LAMBERT D. LE MAIRE

PHOTOGRAPHER: A. L. KNOWLTON-SCHEN

95 FOOD, FUN, AND FRIENDS *When "Corine entertains after dancing
class" grapes are cut in bunches for individual servings and festooned on a pleasing pattern of eucalyptus and lemon leaves which remains attractive when fruit
is eaten. Hot cocoa accompanies sandwiches served from the large white platter
and marshmallows from the nappy. Dishes are white Wedgewood embossed with
a garland of blue grapes; cloth is blue-gray with white applique.*

ARRANGER: MRS. ALFRED S. GRUSSNER.   PHOTOGRAPHER: A. L. KNOWLTON-SCHEN

96 GOODBYE TO FRIENDS OFF TO THE TROPICS As *bon voyage*
decoration, this hostess informally decorates with palm and broccoli, highlighted
with chartreuse-to-yellow mahonia blossoms. A pottery giraffe head (chartreuse)
and bamboo raft add atmosphere. The container is copper. On a mahogany table,
green place mats are recommended.

ARRANGER: MRS. ERHARD ALLEN.   PHOTOGRAPHER: PAUL K. HORN

LEARN SOURCES OF IDEAS

First, you must have an idea to develop a distinctively unusual table. Where can you get it? One source certainly lies in facts and fancies connected with "the kindly fruits of the earth." I confess that my interest in mythology and folklore has been profitable and fascinating. Some references that deserve interpretation have already been made, in Plate 2 for example. Concentrated emphasis will stimulate your imagination as nothing else can do.

THE BABY SHOWER

There are many stories about babies that are pure fancy. In Europe, for example, you may be told that babies are found in cabbages. Nothing would be more arresting on the party table for mother-to-be than a lovely red-purple cabbage with tiny dolls or small angel figurines within the head. To hold them, quarter a cabbage head, cutting almost completely through the center, and submerge it upside down in ice-cold water. After a short while, it will spread to make "pockets."

BIRTHDAY PARTIES

Symbolism is always inspirational. Honor a day of birth with astrological significance. The scale is the sign of justice for the September-born (Plate 77). Such would suit the Friday individual as well, for according to a familiar verse, "Friday's child is loving and giving." Scale symbolism represents his sharing character (Plate 72).

INTERPRETATION

Ideas also lie in facts. Plate 100 is an interpretation of merit. While rice is not fruit or vegetable in the popular sense, it is an edible part of a plant, and thus adaptable to this type of decoration. On this remarkable buffet in tones of tan and brown, the grain harvester ties his ceramic bundle of rice similar to the real sheaf in the background. Bands of headed rice follow the lines of the figure and the

97   FOR THE UNEXPECTED CELLAR PARTY   *No longer than it takes the coffee to percolate this "emergency" decoration was assembled. Nothing but apples and house plant foliage in driftwood on slate results in this compelling decoration against painted concrete walls.*
ARRANGER: MRS. ARTHUR P. ZUCK.   PHOTOGRAPHER: BRYAN STUDIO

98 AN IMPROMPTU BREAKFAST DECORATION *When time does not permit planning, make the most of what is available. Here a green glass candy dish holds a pleasant design with hemlock from the yard, leaves from a house plant begonia, and red grapes from the refrigerator. High placement of the latter can be supported on bare twigs easily concealed by the plant material.*
ARRANGER: MRS. LOUIS H. AMER.   PHOTOGRAPHER: CARPENTER'S STUDIO

99 PANEL DECORATION *A tall slender design as here is just right to bring
interest to a narrow wall space in your dining room. Red grapes hang over the
lip of a bronze vase along the narrow neck to tie the bulbous body to the area
of plant material for beauty that comes with relatedness. Sickle pears, leucothoe,
and lopezia complete the picture.*
ARRANGER: MRS. JAMES L. FINCH.   PHOTOGRAPHER: BOUTRELLE

100   THE STORY OF RICE   *In submitting details concerning this entry in a flower show of the Crowley, Louisiana Garden Club, Mrs. Vincent Daigle, chairman at the time, explained that practically all members participated in bringing the table into reality. Description is on page 114.*
PHOTOGRAPHER: AL ALLEMAN

carborundum stone base. Fungi with its undulating color pattern calls to mind a ripened rice field rippling in the breeze. The candleholders are triers, which are used to remove a few grains from a filled milling bag for testing variety and quality; the burlap cloth is significant of the bags themselves. The candles are handmade to secure a tone to echo that of the grain. The napkins match in hue and are harmonious in texture. A wooden bottle is to hold coffee as it did originally for the laborers; the "cups" are carborundum disks employed in shelling rice. Plates, glasses, bowls are of dark and natural wood; the brown earthenware casserole rests in a wooden support.

A THEME UNIFIES

A theme around which to design a table can always help in conceiving an original aspect which in turn may achieve great distinction in results. For clarification, refer to Plates 44, 64, 65, 76, and 96. While each decoration was planned to satisfy the requirements of a special and personal problem, together they represent a collection that could be interpretive of a single theme—Faraway Places. Each holds something of this common denominator.

Among picture captions in this book are some that present a workable theme. Perhaps the most interesting are included in the following: The Carnival Spirit, Tropicana, Vacation Memories, Gay and Springlike, "Oh, What a Beautiful Morning," Peace and Plenty, "When Good Fellows Get Together."

KEEP YOUR ARRANGEMENTS INDIVIDUAL

The following brief descriptive comments are not final, only suggestive and explanatory. The attractive, practical, and ingenious decorations shared with you through the pages of this book should not be an end, only a beginning. Study them thoughtfully to understand better why they please your eye, but strive to make your own decoration individual. Do not copy. Instead, use the plates to conjure up ideas that are your own and suited to your taste, your experience and your expectation. Above all, have fun while you decorate!

As stimulation to ideas, both truth and fiction are offered in the glossary which follows.

GLOSSARY OF FRUITS,

VEGETABLES, GRAINS

FRUITS

	DECORATIVE CUE	SEASON AND LASTING QUALITY
Apple	Emblem of Aphrodite, Grecian Venus; associated with Johnny Appleseed; literally "fit for a king" as Winesaps are shipped to Europe for use on royal tables	Yearly supply; keeps well
Apricot	Native to Asia; introduced into Europe during time of Alexander the Great; cultivated in England in sixteenth century	June-August; perishable
Avocado (alligator pear)	"Salad fruit of the tropics"; native from Peru to Mexico	Yearly supply; plentiful in fall and winter

Banana (white and red)	Beginning lost in history; technically a berry; rhythmic order of placement in the "hand" is suggestive of long yellow flower petals	Fully ripe fruit is perishable; green-tipped will keep from 3 to 6 days; yearly supply
Blueberry	Most widely distributed fruit in the world although cultivated only in United States and Canada	July-August
Carambola	"Starfruit" of Florida	Ripens at intervals throughout the year
Coconut	Symbol of endless summer; seed distributed by ocean drifting, so establishes itself in all warm climates; available in green, yellow, and bright orange as well as familiar brown	Long keeping quality
Citron	Symbol of happiness	Keeps well
Cranberry	Typically American; 90 per cent of total crop harvested in Massachusetts, especially in Cape Cod area	Shrivels in 5 to 7 days; September-February
Fig	Symbol of life	Extremely perishable
Grape	Best known of all berries; wine grapes brought to America by Columbus; symbol of abundance, pleasure, good cheer, unity (cluster); emblem of mythological wine gods, Dionysus and Bacchus	Yearly season; skin toughness of Tokay variety makes them rugged for decorative use
Grapefruit	So called because it grows in clusters like grapes; many believe it to be ancient pomelo	Keeps well for at least 2 weeks; September-August
Lemon	Native to northern India	Keeps well for at least 2 weeks; yearly supply
Mango	Golden-red delicacy; one of world's most important fruits; sacred in India; cultivated in California and Florida	Not long keeping

Melons	Varieties impressive: cantaloupe, casaba, Cranshaw, honey ball, honeydew, watermelon, Christmas or Santa Claus melon	Christmas melon, best keeper of winter group
Orange	"Celestial fruit"; symbolizes marriage	Keeps at least 2 weeks; yearly supply
Papaw	"Poor man's banana" or "custard apple" (has custard-like pulp and resembles stubby banana); native to Ozark region in United States; green-yellow when ripe; turns brown a few days after pulled	In New York markets in the fall
Papaya	Orange-gold; high in vitamin C content	Keeps 3 to 5 days in ripened stage
Peach	Symbol of long life	Perishable; May-October
Pear	Symbol of human heart; available in brown, green, pink, blush-red; no fruit compares in aroma or range of flavors	Bruises easily in handling; July-March
Persimmon	Symbol of wisdom; Chinese variety cultivated in the South	Marketed in October; fairly good keeper
Pineapple	"King of fruits"; derives name from old English word, pinappel, meaning pine cone, which it resembles in shape and surface pattern; available in brown, orange, and rosy tones; symbol of hospitality	Keeps approximately 5 days
Plum	Symbolizes longevity of life, like the peach	Perishable
Pomegranate	Old World companion to date and fig; associated in mythology with Persephone; its numerous seeds gave rise to symbolism of abundance, fruitfulness, and pagan man's belief that it was a "gift from the gods"	Keeps well

Prickly pear	"Indian fig"; resembles prickly pear cactus which grows in sand or among rocks	Good keeper
Tangerine	A variety of orange, the mandarin	Keeps 5 to 7 days
Strawberry	Associated with many legends and myths; one of the loveliest connects it with Frigga, the Norse goddess of spring	Perishable

VEGETABLES

Artichoke (globe or French)	Member of thistle family; given particular attention in Egypt as a product brought back from plant-collecting expeditions in eighteenth dynasty; develops into large decorative violet flowers	Perishable; pick buds early for eating
Bean	Staple food for generations; in early days, limas or "butter beans" were kept in storage to be used by travelers	Wilts in a few days; yearly supply
Cabbage	Has legendary associations; Savoy distinguished by very crinkly leaves	Keeps well; yearly supply
Cauliflower	Pride of cabbage clan	Purple strain easy to grow, but not generally marketed because it bruises easily; white is marketed all year
Chard	Swiss chard or "silver beet" was cultivated by ancients; rhubarb chard, distinguished by red stalks and veins in dark green leaves, is a Swiss chard of comparatively recent cultivation; tropical in effect	Wilts readily

Corn	Symbol of wealth; most important of all New World plants; cultivated by Indians; strawberry popcorn, 1½-by-2-inch mahogany-red ears	Keeps well for decorative purpose, though it has a fleeting moment of taste perfection
Cucumber	Edible gourd containing a cooling property responsible for the phrase, "as cool as a cucumber"	Yearly supply except in January
Eggplant	"Mad apple," a tropical berry of the poisonous nightshade family	Yearly supply
Kohlrabi	Member of cabbage family	Usually home-grown; seldom marketed
Lettuce	Appreciated long before Christian Era; universally grown	Wilts readily; yearly supply
Mushroom	An edible fungus; "buttons" are baby mushrooms	Browns in 2 days
Okra (gumbo)	Favored in South for soup; a tropical vegetable, but will grow anywhere its flower-garden cousin, the hollyhock, survives; one of the most ornamental of vegetable plants; in African legend, it was once the child in the moon	Keeps well
Onion	Important even in ancient times; scallion is grandparent of leek, national emblem of Wales	Keeps well; yearly supply
Parsnip	Nutritious herb	One of the few root crops that can remain in ground all winter; frost improves flavor
Pea	Symbol of romance	April-November
Pepper	During his momentous voyage, Columbus found red peppers used by Indians; tobacco pepper, long, red, hot to the taste;	Keeps well; yearly supply

chili and cayenne peppers are threaded on strings and dried before sold in market; sweet green pepper, a berry of the nightshade family

Potato (white and sweet)	Native of Chile, Peru, and Rocky Mountains of North America; introduced into England from America in sixteenth century; grown by the Irish when grain crops failed in eighteenth century and became so popular that the white was named "Irish potato"	White keeps well; yearly supply. Sweet, October-May
Radish	Important in ancient China, Japan, Egypt; English call the all-red strain "red coal" because of stringent taste	Keeps at least a week
Rhubarb	"Pieplant," closely related to common dock, having attractively crumpled leaves	Wilts readily
Rutabaga	Swedish version of turnip	Keeps well
Squash	A gourd; served at first Thanksgiving in Plymouth	Winter varieties keep well
Tomato	"Love apple" of yesteryear; of New World origin; cultivated by Indians; berry of nightshade family	Perishable; April-December

GRAINS

Oats	Symbolizes the enchanting spirit of music
Rice	"Bread and potatoes" of Middle East countries
Wheat	One of three oldest grains known to civilization; symbolizes the Staff of Life

INDEX